"These books will make super resources [...] thoughtful church leaders, and indeed f[...] their faith, and its ecumenical history, se[...]"

CARL R. TRUEMAN, Paul [...] [...]. Church History, Westminster Theological Seminary, PA

"Faithful wisdom through the centuries needs to be explored for our own engagement with Scripture today. It takes a gifted scholar to survey these sources well and a gifted teacher to communicate them to the person in the pew. Justin Holcomb is that sort of scholar-communicator."

MICHAEL HORTON, J. G. Machen Professor of Systematic Theology and Apologetics, Westminster Seminary, CA; author, *The Christian Faith*

"I welcome the Know series as an important companion in our lifelong quest to know God better."

CAROLYN CUSTIS JAMES, author, *When Life and Beliefs Collide*

"The Know series gives local leaders and churches short, succinct, accurate, theologically informed, and relevant sketches of big topics in theology. Pastors and professors will discover they are unable to keep students from these volumes."

SCOT MCKNIGHT, author, *King Jesus Gospel*

"Jesus promised that the Spirit would lead the church into truth. That means that history matters. These concise books from Justin Holcomb are invitations into that history, to see how the Spirit led the church to articulate the orthodox Christian faith and how that scriptural imagination helped them discern errors and wrong turns. We need this wisdom more than ever in our postmodern moment."

JAMES K. A. SMITH, Gary and Henrietta Byker Chair in Applied Reformed Theology and Worldview, Calvin College; author, *Letters to a Young Calvinist* and *Desiring the Kingdom*

"With pastoral insight and historical integrity, Dr. Holcomb has provided us with an accessible handbook on the major heretics and heresies of the church. Holcomb not only helps to unravel the ancient heresies of the church but also shows how they relate to similar heresies in our own day."

BURK PARSONS, copastor, Saint Andrew's Chapel

"Why do we need to know the heretics? In this brief, balanced, and readable volume, Justin Holcomb shows that the old heresies keep coming back or never quite go away. His book is an informative introduction to ancient heresy and orthodoxy, and provides necessary weapons for combating their contemporary permutations."

PETER LEITHART, President, Trinity House, Birmingham, AL; author, *Against Christianity* and *Defending Constantine*

"I applaud the Know series in its effort to equip the saints; I encourage pastors and laypeople alike to diligently read these books."

JAMES H. GILMORE, coauthor, *The Experience Economy*

Books in the Know Series

Know the Creeds and Councils
Know the Heretics

KNOW
THE
HERETICS

JUSTIN S. HOLCOMB

ZONDERVAN

Know the Heretics
Copyright © 2014 by Justin Holcomb

This title is also available as a Zondervan ebook.

Requests for information should be addressed to:

Zondervan, 3900 *Sparks Drive SE, Grand Rapids, Michigan 49546*

Library of Congress Cataloging-in-Publication Data

Holcomb, Justin S.
    Know the heretics / Justin S. Holcomb.
       pages cm.— (The know series)
    Includes bibliographical references.
    ISBN 978-0-310-51507-4 (softcover)
    1. Christian heresies. 2. Christian heretics. I. Title.
BT1315.3.H65 2014
273—dc23   2013049100

Cover design: Gearbox
Interior composition: Greg Johnson/Textbook Perfect

First printing April 2014 / Printed in the United States of America

CONTENTS

FOREWORD

Why try to understand the heretics? We learn something important from them: how to distinguish the apostolic teaching from those views of Scripture that are not consistent with original Christianity. The heretics warn us not to be deceived by well-meaning teachers who have not listened carefully enough to Scripture to articulate the faith as understood by the apostles. Classic Christian writers have pointed to God's purpose for permitting heresies: to awaken the church to misinterpretations of the apostles' intentions.

In *Know the Heretics*, Justin Holcomb has condensed a great deal of complex information into concise, well-informed, and simple explanations of why these ideas are "other than" (*hairesis*) that which has been consensually received by the major interpreters of the apostolic tradition over the largest possible time frame.

—Thomas C. Oden

ACKNOWLEDGMENTS

First of all, a special thanks to Jeffrey Haines for his superb research assistance and editing. Much gratitude for those who also assisted with research: Jordan Buckley, James Gordon, Nathan Chang.

I would like to thank Carl Trueman for his insights and advice on how to approach the history of heretics and heresies.

At Zondervan, I would like to thank my editor, Madison Trammel, who supported the book and series marvelously.

INTRODUCTION

Why Heresy?

> The orthodox Church never took the tame course or accepted
> the conventions; the orthodox Church was never respectable
> … It is always easier to let the age have its head; the difficult
> thing is to keep one's own.
>
> — G. K. Chesterton, Orthodoxy

Who is Jesus? Is he divine? Is he human? How does he relate to
the God of the Old Testament? How do the divinity and humanity of Christ relate to his work in saving humanity? How is the fact
that Christ was both human and God connected to how he rescues
humanity? What does that rescue look like? How does Jesus save —
by example or by some supernatural intervention?

These are the questions that the leaders and thinkers of the early
church wrestled with after the time of the apostles. And as you might
imagine, the answers were far from clear-cut. Over the course of the
first few centuries, a large number of theories were developed to try
to explain all that the Bible has to say about God and humanity. But
not all of these explanations were equally well grounded — many of
them owed too much to the spirit of the times or cut out essential

parts of the Bible in order to make the explanation fit. This book is the story of those theories — what they were and why they did not become a part of mainstream Christianity. Some believe that these theories were rejected because the institutional church was unwilling to be open minded; however, although I have tried to represent them as fairly as possible here, I am taking the position that they were rejected because they simply did not measure up to the beliefs that were accepted in the end.

The main terms I will use throughout this book for the different sides are "orthodoxy," for the mainstream doctrines, and "heresy," for the theories that were not accepted.

What Is Orthodoxy?

Orthodoxy (literally "right teaching") is the word that most scholars use for mainstream Christianity. But as you might imagine, every group thinks that it has the right teaching! What's more, the groups that we will be describing as orthodox were not always those who had the support of the institutional church, the smartest thinkers, or the greatest influence. During the Arian controversy (chapter 7), for instance, not only did most of the clergy take the heretical side but the state persecuted the group that we are going to refer to as orthodox. A similar thing happened during the Monothelite controversy, when the heresy was contained to a small group but happened to include the emperor and the highest church officials. So orthodoxy and heresy can't be measured by the number of bishops or intellectuals — or numbers, period — who embraced a given theory.

Because we aren't basing our definitions of orthodoxy on how these groups viewed themselves or on an objective category like number of supporters, a cynical interpretation might be that orthodoxy is the teaching that succeeded and heresy the teaching that lost out. In this view, modern Christianity is more or less an accident. We believe that certain theories are better not because they are truer but because we happen to have inherited them. (Much like saying that if a Christian had been born in India, he would have been a Hindu; if Arianism had won out, we would all be Arians and think that Arianism was more faithful to the Bible.) We'll come back to this view in a bit, because it deserves a detailed response, but suffice it to say that I believe that God is active in the world and is interested in preserving his revelation, his truth, and his church, even though his revelation may be misunderstood or ignored, the truth may be doubted or questioned, and his church may go through some dark and puzzling times.

In the end, I will define orthodoxy as follows. Orthodoxy is the teaching that best follows the Bible and best summarizes what it teaches — best accounts for the paradoxes and apparent contradictions, best preserves the mystery of God in the places where reason can't go, and best communicates the story of the forgiveness of the gospel. For each heresy that we discuss, I will try to demonstrate why the orthodox position best accounts for the Bible's teaching and why it was a good thing that the church chose it.

What Is Heresy?

Heresy can be a fighting word. Traditionally, a heretic is someone who has compromised an essential doctrine and lost sight of who God really is, usually by oversimplification. Literally, heresy means "choice" — that is, a choice to deviate from traditional teaching in favor of one's own insights. But that sense of the word has been lost. To some people today, heretic suggests a rebel — someone with courage, the kind of person who can think for himself and stand up to the institutional church. Some Christians simply use the word to refer to anyone who doesn't agree with their particular version of Christianity. In modern parlance, the word heretic usually means that you aren't in the club, but it's not the sort of club you would want to be in anyway.

There have been times when the church has taken extreme measures to punish innocent dissidents by labeling them heretics. Even so, giving heresy a positive meaning is worrisome. The concept of heresy is a valid one. It's true that the church has often been too quick to brand a new leader or idea as heretical, sometimes to its later embarrassment — the way that the Catholic Church handled Galileo's idea that the earth revolves around the sun is a classic example — but in many instances, a legitimate heresy has threatened to confuse ordinary believers simply because of the speculations of an influential thinker. It is often a fine balance between allowing free exploration of who God is and reasserting what we can know for sure, and in the cases presented in this book, the exploration went so far as to distort our understanding of God as he has revealed himself to us.

This book is a case study of fourteen major events when the church made the right call — not for political or status reasons (though politics and status sometimes played a part) but because orthodox teaching preserved Jesus' message in the best sense, and the new teaching distorted it.

As Christianity grew and spread, it increasingly came into contact with competing belief systems such as paganism, Greek philosophy, Gnosticism, and others. Inevitably, teachers arose who attempted to solve the intellectual difficulties of Christian faith and make it more compatible with other philosophical systems. In this way, many of the heresies that arose had to do with the identity of Jesus Christ as he related to the God of Israel.

It should be made clear that most of those dubbed heretics were usually asking legitimate and important questions. They weren't heretics because they asked the questions. It is the answers that they gave that are wrong. They went too far by trying to make the Christian faith more compatible with ideas that they already found appealing, especially those of pagan Greek philosophy. Others struggled with Jesus' claims to be both sent from God and one with God. The reactions of the religious leaders in the New Testament to Jesus' claims underline the difficulty of this revelation and point to later struggles about Jesus' identity.

The following briefly describes the answers given by some of the thinkers we will cover in more detail in this book:

Marcion: The God of the Old Testament and Jesus in the New Testament are two different gods.

Docetists: Jesus only appeared to be human.

Arius: The Son was a created being of a lower order than the Father.

Apollinarius: Jesus' divine nature/*Logos* replaced the human rational soul in the incarnation. In other words, Jesus' "pure" divine nature replaced the "filthy" mind of a typical human.

Sabellius: Jesus and the Father are not distinct but just "modes" of a single being.

Eutyches: The divinity of Christ overwhelms his humanity.

Nestorius: Jesus was composed of two separate persons, one divine and one human.

Whereas orthodox Christianity answers Jesus' question to Peter — "Who do you say I am?" (Mark 8:29) — by affirming that Christ was both God (the Creator of the universe, the Lord of Israel) and human (an average Joe, yet without sin), these heretical thinkers answered the question differently. As we will see, their challenges caused a tragic amount of controversy among Christians in the early centuries of the church. However, with each new heresy, the church was forced to study the Scriptures, wrestle with intellectual problems, and articulate more clearly the "faith which was once for all delivered to the saints" (Jude 3 RSV).

Does the Bible Mention Heresy?

The Bible itself seems to presuppose a right and a wrong interpretation of Jesus' coming and the nature and character of God, as it uses strong language against false teachers who promote doctrines that undermine the gospel. As historical theologian Bruce Demarest notes, "the NT expresses serious concern for 'false doctrines' (1 Tim. 1:3; 6:3) and places the highest priority on maintaining 'the pattern of sound teaching' (2 Tim. 1:13; cf. 1 Tim. 6:3). Scripture urges Christians to be alert to doctrinal deception (Mt. 24:4) and to avoid heresy by carefully guarding the pure content of the gospel (1 Cor. 11:2; Gal. 1:8)."[1]

In Galatians 1:9, Paul uses the strongest words possible against those who distort the gospel, writing, "If anybody is preaching to you a gospel other than what you accepted, let them be under God's curse!" And the apostle Peter warns against "false teachers among you [who] will secretly introduce destructive heresies, even denying the sovereign Lord who bought them — bringing swift destruction on themselves" (2 Peter 2:1).

As is clear from the New Testament, the apostles were not afraid to call out heresy when they saw it. If a teaching or practice threatened the integrity of the gospel, it was strongly condemned (as in the case of Peter and the circumcision party described in Galatians 2). However, heresy was a weighty charge that was not made lightly, nor was it used whenever there was theological inaccuracy or imprecision. (Think of the response to Apollos in Acts 18:24 – 28.)

Heresy and the Early Church

Following the apostles, the early church maintained that heresy means directly denying the central orthodox beliefs of the church. Early church creedal statements codified orthodoxy into a widely accepted form. Even before important Christian beliefs such as the canon of Scripture (list of books in the Bible) and the Trinity had been carefully articulated, the mainstream of Christian believers and leaders had a sense of the essential truths that had been handed down from the apostles and the prophets, and passed along to each generation of Christians through Scripture, sermons, and baptismal creeds. Before the developments at Nicaea and Chalcedon regarding the proper beliefs about the Trinity and the dual natures of Christ, the early church possessed what is known as the "rule of faith." To quote Demarest again, "The early church defended itself against heretical teaching by appealing to 'the rule of faith' or 'the rule of truth', which were brief summaries of essential Christian truths … The fluid 'rule of faith' gave way to more precise instruments for refuting heresies and defining faith, namely, creedal formulations such as the Apostles' Creed, the Nicene Creed, the Definition of Chalcedon and the Athanasian Creed."[2]

The New Testament speaks frequently about false teaching and doctrine. For the early church, heresy was merely teaching that stood in contrast to the right belief received from the prophets and the apostles in the Scriptures and put into written formulas in the rule of faith and the creeds. The early church formed an accepted and received statement of what is true and essential to the Christian faith. The rule of faith gave birth to more precise statements of the essentials of the faith, such as the Apostles' Creed and the Nicene Creed.[3] These widely accepted formulations of the essential "right doctrine" (orthodoxy) handed down from the apostles were crucial for combating heresy.

It is important to note, however, that the early church did not consider every potential wrong belief to be heretical. Rather, only those beliefs that contradicted the essential elements of the faith were to be labeled heresy, not disagreements on nonessential doctrines.

Unlike some churches today, the early church did not stipulate all of the minor beliefs that its members should hold, nor did it consider mere disagreement to be heresy. Significant leaders in the early church wrote about heresy as a corruption of right doctrine rather than merely an alternative point of view:

Origen: "All heretics are at first believers; then later they deviate from the rule of faith."[4]

Irenaeus urged Christians "to avoid every heretical, godless and impious doctrine."[5]

Tertullian said that "to know nothing in opposition to the rule of faith is to know all things."[6] He also said that "the philosophers are the fathers of the heretics."[7]

Clement of Alexandria said that heresies are a result of self-deceit and a mishandling of the Scriptures.[8]

Cyprian said, "Satan invented heresies and schisms with which to overthrow the faith, to corrupt the truth and to divide unity."[9]

Not All Theological Errors Are Equally Serious

Because there is always some room for mystery and speculation, both the Roman Catholic and Reformed traditions have been careful to distinguish three "zones" between strict orthodoxy and outright heresy. In Catholicism, to bluntly deny an explicitly defined church doctrine is heresy in the first degree — for example, a severe contradiction, like saying that Christ is not God. A doctrine that has not been explicitly defined by one of the church's articles of faith but diverges from the received majority view is considered an opinion approaching heresy (*sententia haeresi proxima*) — for instance, to say that Christ can be found in other religions. One who holds a position that does not directly contradict received tradition but logically denies an explicitly defined truth is said to be erroneous in theology (*propositio theologice erronea*). Finally, a belief that cannot be definitively shown to be in opposition to an article of faith of the church is said to be suspected or savoring of heresy (*sententia de haeresi suspecta, haeresim sapiens*).[10]

Similarly, the Reformed tradition has traditionally distinguished three kinds of doctrinal error related to fundamental articles of the faith:[11] (1) errors directly against a fundamental article (*contra fundamentum*); (2) errors around a fundamental or in indirect contradiction to it (*circa fundamentum*); (3) errors beyond a fundamental article (*praeter fundamentum*).

The point is that historically both the Roman Catholic tradition and the Reformed tradition have understood that not all theological errors are equally serious. Theological historian David Christie-Murray distinguishes between orthodoxy, the body of Christian belief which has emerged as a consensus through time as the church reflects on Scripture; heterodoxy, Christian belief which differs from orthodoxy; and heresy, belief that diverges from orthodoxy beyond a certain point.[12]

It is important to bear these distinctions in mind as we discuss heresy, since there are those who think that heresy is anything that does not agree with their own interpretation of Holy Scripture. These people fail to differentiate between the primary and secondary elements of the Christian faith and make every belief they have into a pillar of Christianity. So, on this view, if someone disagrees with them about the millennium, about infant baptism, about the role of women in ministry, or about the nature of the atonement, they are quickly labeled a heretic. While such impulses can be well intentioned, sometimes because Scripture reveals a great deal about God's workings, the church of the New Testament walked the line between holding fast to some convictions and being flexible about others.

Though this group of heresy-hunters often say they're motivated by concern for the faith once for all delivered to the saints, their practice of labeling every diverging belief as heresy has the opposite effect. Rather than making much of right belief, they minimize its importance by making, for example, the mode of baptism to be as important as the divinity of Christ. When everything is central, nothing is.

Is It Even Appropriate to Speak of Heresy?

In a modern, pluralistic society, it can be hard to imagine a "wrong" or "dangerous" interpretation of a religion, as long as it does not encourage violence or hurt to others. This is particularly true when it comes to a book like the Bible, which everyone agrees has a few parts that are difficult to understand. For this reason, more and more scholars are arguing that it is no longer appropriate to speak of heresy and orthodoxy in the early church. Instead, they argue, there were a number of early Christian groups who all took Jesus' words to mean different things. According to this theory, the Christianity that modern people practice is simply the descendant of one of these early groups that happened to win out — the other early Christian groups are heretical from *its* point of view, but from *their* point of view modern Christianity would be heretical. (This is a scholarly version of the historical accident view mentioned in the section on orthodoxy.)

This idea was most famously promoted by Walter Bauer, a twentieth-century scholar of early Christianity who wrote about his theory in *Orthodoxy and Heresy in Earliest Christianity* in 1934. Bauer argued that there was really no such thing as objective heresy in the early church. Rather, according to his thesis, the Roman church labeled its own view of Christian doctrine orthodoxy while calling others who did not hold to their own views heretical. Bauer argued that these heretical forms of Christianity actually preceded so-called orthodoxy. According to him, there were many early Christian movements that we know of today as heretical that were actually practicing some form or another of legitimate expression of devotion to Christ. Thus, heresy is not a concept to be viewed in contrast to truth or right doctrine; rather heresy is any view that opposes the political interests of the church and as such needs to be stamped out.[13] Orthodoxy is merely that which has been advanced by the Roman church as correct in order to facilitate some sort of oppressive control over those who would thwart their expansive efforts.

There is much to be said against this view. Bauer's thesis has been shown time and time again to be false. In reaction to Bauer, Canon H. E. W. Turner argued in his book *The Pattern of Christian Truth* that early Christians held to three fixed, nonnegotiable elements of faith: (1) religious facts such as God the creator and the divine historical redeemer Christ; (2) the centrality of biblical revelation; and (3) the creed and the rule of faith.[14] That is, early

Christians, though marred by sin and susceptible to error, were ultimately concerned with truth about God, not politics.

In fact, it is the historical redeemer (rather than myth), the centrality of the Bible (over pagan philosophy), and the traditional creed (rather than innovation) that distinguished the orthodox from the heretics. An important question regarding heresy is whether there is really a tradition that leads back to Jesus Christ. The ancient Christians took great pains to establish such a connection; they were interested not simply in propagandizing other groups but in upholding what they believed to be their authentic inheritance, based on real events that had made a difference in the world. "To my mind," Ignatius of Antioch declared less than a century after Christ, "it is Jesus Christ who is the original documents. The inviolable archives are his cross and death and his resurrection and the faith that came by him. It is by these things and by your prayers that I want to be justified."[15] It was vital for Ignatius and others like him to preserve the story of Christ as it had been passed down to them. As will be seen, most heretical groups were not particularly interested in doing likewise.

Why Do We Need to Learn about Heresy?

Core Christian doctrines such as the Trinity, the nature of Christ, and which books should be included in Scripture were developed through the early church's struggles with heresy.[16] When teachers began to lead movements that were blatantly opposed to the apostolic tradition, the church was forced to articulate the essential elements of the faith.

The history of heretics, heresies, and the orthodox leaders who responded to them can be disheartening. Why learn about arguments over what sometimes seems like theological minutiae? There are two major reasons. The first is that while there is certainly ambiguity in the Bible, the Creator of the world has decided to reveal himself to us and even to live with us. It is important to honor that revelation. When we find this revelation distasteful and try to reshape God according to our preferences, we are beginning to drift away from God as he really is. Imagine a friend who ignores the parts of you that he or she doesn't like. Is that a deep relationship? Ambiguity or not, uncomfortable or not, it is vital that we are obedient to what we *can* know about God.

The second reason is related to the first. When we have a flawed image of God, we no longer relate to him in the same way. Think of the way that you might have related to your parents when you were growing up. Even if you didn't necessarily understand the reasons behind boundaries they set for you in childhood, they look a lot different when you are confident in your parents' love than when you fear or resent your parents. It is surprising how much our beliefs about God impact our daily lives, which is partly what makes theology such a rewarding (although difficult and dangerous) discipline.

It cannot be repeated enough that (as the old cliche goes) those who forget history are doomed to repeat it. Moreover, as C. S. Lewis warns, if we remain ignorant of the errors and triumphs of our history, we run the risk of what he calls "chronological snobbery," the arrogant assumption that the values and beliefs of our own time have surpassed all that came before. Lewis writes, "We need intimate knowledge of the past. Not that the past has any magic about it, but because we cannot study the future, and yet need something to set against the present, to remind us that the basic assumptions have been quite different in different periods and that much which seems certain to the uneducated is merely temporary fashion. A man who has lived in many places is not likely to be deceived by the local errors of his native village; the scholar has lived in many times and is therefore in some degree immune from the great cataract of nonsense that pours from the press and the microphone of his own age."[17]

Learning how Christians throughout history have wrestled with the tough questions of our faith gives us a valuable perspective and keeps us from assuming that our own know-how, pat answers, or inspiring platitudes are best suited to solving the problems of the world.

Know the Heretics

This book aims to provide an accessible overview of some of the major heresies throughout the Christian tradition. It is not intended as a comprehensive guide to *all* heresies — there are far too many for anything less than an encyclopedia to cover them all. Nor is this book meant to offer any kind of systematic theory of the nature of heresy and orthodoxy. Rather, I hope that after reading this book you will come away with a greater understanding of the main heretical figures and ideas that have most impacted the history of Christianity.

This book is designed to be read by individuals or used in a group setting. My hope is that this book will complement longer works such as Alister McGrath's *Heresy: A History of Defending the Truth*. His book is about heresy in general and touches only briefly on specific heresies and heretics.

The chapters are brief and to the point. For each heretic, I present the historical background, the heretical teaching, the orthodox response, and contemporary relevance. Because some readers will prefer to look at just a few specific issues, I have tried to strike a balance between letting each chapter stand alone and building the narrative of the "progression of doctrine." Recommended reading for further study and discussion questions are included at the end of each chapter.

Further Reading on Heretics and Heresies

Bromiley, Geoffrey. *Historical Theology: An Introduction.* Grand Rapids, MI: Eerdmans, 1978.

Brown, Harold O. J. *Heresies: Heresies and Orthodoxy in the History of the Church.* Peabody, MA: Hendrickson, 2003.

Chadwick, Henry. *The Early Church.* Rev. ed. New York: Penguin, 1993.

Davis, Leo Donald. *The First Seven Ecumenical Councils (325–787): Their History and Theology.* Collegeville, MN: Liturgical Press, 1983.

Frend, W. H. C. *The Rise of Christianity.* Philadelphia: Fortress, 1984.

Kelly, J. N. D. *Early Christian Doctrines.* Rev. ed. San Francisco: HarperCollins, 1978.

Kostenberger, Andreas, Michael J. Kruger, and I. Howard Marshall. *The Heresy of Orthodoxy: How Contemporary Culture's Fascination with Diversity Has Reshaped Our Understanding of Early Christianity.* Wheaton, IL: Crossway, 2010.

McGrath, Alistair E. *Heresy: A History of Defending the Truth.* New York: HarperOne, 2010.

———. *Historical Theology: An Introduction to the History of Christian Thought.* Malden, MA: Blackwell, 1998.

Nichols, Stephen J. *For Us and for Our Salvation: The Doctrine of Christ in the Early Church.* Wheaton, IL: Crossway, 2007.

Olson, Roger E. *The Story of Christian Theology: Twenty Centuries of Tradition and Reform.* Downers Grove, IL: InterVarsity Academic, 1999.

Pelikan, Jaroslav. *The Emergence of the Catholic Tradition (100–600).* Vol. 1 of *The Christian Tradition: A History of the Development of Doctrine.* Chicago: Univ. of Chicago Press, 1971.

Quash, Ben, and Michael Ward. *Heresies and How to Avoid Them: Why It Matters What Christians Believe.* Grand Rapids, MI: Baker Academic, 2007.

Schaff, Philip. *History of the Christian Church.* Vol. 2. 1858; Peabody, MA: Hendrickson, 2006.

Schaff, Philip and Henry Wace, eds. *Ante-Nicene Fathers.* Vol. 1. Reprint. Peabody, MA: Hendrickson, 1995.

———. *Ante-Nicene Fathers.* Vol. 3. Reprint. Peabody, MA: Hendrickson, 1995.

———. *Nicene and Post-Nicene Fathers: First Series.* Vol. 5. Reprint. Peabody, MA: Hendrickson, 1995.

———. *Nicene and Post-Nicene Fathers: Second Series.* Vol. 4. Translated by Cardinal Newman. Reprint. Peabody, MA: Hendrickson, 1995.

CHAPTER 1

JUDAIZERS

The Old Rules Still Apply

Historical Background

One of the earliest heresies in the church is known only from the New Testament. As everyone knows, Jesus was a Jewish man, and most of his early followers were Jewish as well. In fact, there are some statements that suggest that his mission was a purely Jewish affair; for instance, consider how he says, "Do not think that I have come to abolish the Law or the Prophets; I have not come to abolish them but to fulfill them" (Matt. 5:17), and, "I was sent only to the lost sheep of Israel" (Matt. 15:24). But mixed with these Jewish statements are several instances when he heals non-Jews and sends his disciples to spread the message of his coming to the peoples surrounding Israel.

As long as those coming to Christ were circumcised[1] and followed the customs of the Jewish law of the Old Testament, there was no issue about Jewishness or non-Jewishness. But when uncircumcised Gentiles started following Christ, the church became divided on what Christ had intended. Did he mean that Christianity was to be an updated or expanded version of Judaism, in which the laws of the Old Testament were now to be applied to converted non-Jews? If not, what was the connection between Christ and the Old Testament — how could the new followers still be heirs of the promises that God had made to the Jewish people? Certain Jewish believers wanted the Gentiles to be circumcised and to follow Jewish customs if they were to be saved and considered their equals in Christ. These early Jewish Christians have come to be known as the Judaizers.

Heretical Teaching

There are three major incidents with Judaizers in the New Testament. One is the circumcised believers criticizing of Peter for eating with Gentiles (non-Jews) in Acts 11, a second is the first church council in Acts 15, and the last is Paul's opposition of Peter recorded in Galatians 2. From these three incidents, we can gather the basics of the Judaizing heresy.

The first incident occurs in Acts 11. In Acts 10, the apostle Peter receives a vision in which all foods are declared clean, contrary to Jewish law.[2] He interprets this vision to mean that all people, "clean" and "unclean" or "Jew" and "Gentile," are meant to be included in God's kingdom, and the Holy Spirit leads him to the house of a Gentile named Cornelius to put this new plan into practice. However, when Peter returns to Jerusalem from the house of Cornelius, a group known as the "circumcision party" (the Judaizers) is upset with him: "So when Peter went up to Jerusalem, the circumcision party criticized him, saying, 'Why did you go to uncircumcised men and eat with them?'" (Acts 11:2–3 RSV).

The circumcision party seems to be an established group by this point, because the reader is expected to know who they are without any explanation. The criticism that Peter faces here for eating with an uncircumcised believer will reappear later from the other side of the fence; Paul will criticize him for *refusing* to eat with uncircumcised believers.

The second major appearance of the circumcision party comes during the first church council, which is described in Acts 15. In that instance, Paul and Barnabas are in Antioch, where they "gathered the church together and reported all that God had done through them and how he had opened a door of faith to the Gentiles" (Acts 14:27). However, "Certain people came down from Judea to Antioch and were teaching the believers: 'Unless you are circumcised, according to the custom taught by Moses, you cannot be saved.' This brought Paul and Barnabas into sharp dispute and debate with them. So Paul and Barnabas were appointed, along with some other believers, to go up to Jerusalem to see the apostles and elders about this question" (Acts 15:1–2).

Here the ideas of the circumcision party become clearer. In Acts 11, the circumcision party criticizes Peter, but does not explain why eating with an uncircumcised believer is a big deal. In Acts 15, we see that these men who came from Judea specifically connect the act of circumcision with salvation. The Gentiles must be circumcised like Jews or they "cannot be saved" (Greek *sozo*, used for salvation throughout the New Testament). The passage continues with Paul, Barnabas, and the others appointed to accompany them going to Jerusalem to discuss the matter: "When they came to Jerusalem, they were welcomed by the church and the apostles and elders, to whom they reported everything God had done through them. Then some of the believers who belonged to the party of the Pharisees stood up and said, 'The Gentiles must be circumcised and required to keep the law of Moses'" (Acts 15:4–5).

Two things are worth noticing here: circumcision is mentioned again as the prerequisite to salvation, and it is some believers (that is, people inside the church rather than another sect) who were formerly members of the Pharisees who are stirring things up. The circumcision party is openly interested in forcing non-Jewish Christians to observe Jewish customs, with the most prominent customs being those that clearly separated Jews from the surrounding culture: often circumcision, though issues like calendar observances (for example, Sabbath) and food laws seem to be on the agenda as well.

However, the best-known encounter with the circumcision party occurs later, in Galatians, where Paul coins the term "Judaizer." The word Judaizer is found only once in the entire New Testament, in

Galatians 2:14, where Paul rebukes Peter (Cephas) for no longer eating with Gentiles when certain Jews arrive in Antioch. For a traditional Jew, eating with a non-Jew made him "unclean" — not morally evil, but what we might think of as "dirty." Peter is implicitly endorsing the circumcision party, and Paul calls him out: "When I saw that they were not acting in line with the truth of the gospel, I said to Cephas [Peter] in front of them all, 'You are a Jew, yet you live like a Gentile and not like a Jew. How is it, then, that you force Gentiles to follow Jewish customs [in the Greek, "Judaize"]?'" (Gal. 2:14).

Depending on the English version, the underlying word is translated in slightly different ways: "live like Jews" (ESV, NASB), "follow Jewish customs" (NIV), "follow the Jewish traditions" (NLT).[3] However, the gist of the word is the same.[4] It is found in some other literature outside the New Testament, as well, where it indicates living like a Jew.[5] The issue here is not simply that Peter was following his native customs but that he was sending the message that it was following those customs that reconciled Gentiles with God. As one scholar writes, "Paul's opponents were not merely insisting on the nationalization of Gentiles into Israel as a prerequisite for fellowship in the church, but were strenuously insisting that their very salvation rested on obeying the law."[6] Thus, Paul saw Judaizing conduct as "not acting in line with the truth of the gospel" (Gal. 2:14).

But the Judaizers drew their beliefs not from pagan philosophy or exotic religious ideas but from the actions of God in earlier times. God had commanded his chosen people to practice circumcision. He had given them laws that were to mark them out as a chosen people. Had God changed his mind?

Orthodox Response

The determining factor in the orthodox response was that God himself seemed to have discarded the old categories of Jew and non-Jew; furthermore, he had given the church ample indication of this change by giving the Holy Spirit to non-Jews without converting them to Jewish practices first. In Acts 10, when Peter saw that the Holy Spirit "had been poured out even on Gentiles" (v. 45) — none of whom was circumcised — his response was, "So if God gave them the same gift he gave us who believed in the Lord Jesus Christ, who was I to think that I could stand in God's way?" and the response of those to whom he recounted this was to acknowledge, "So then, even to Gentiles God has granted repentance that leads to life" (Acts 11:17–18). Later, at the Council of Jerusalem, Paul makes a similar case: "God, who knows the heart, showed that he accepted them by giving the Holy Spirit to them, just as he did to us. He did not discriminate between us and them, for he purified their hearts by faith" (Acts 15:8–9). Therefore, human opinions had to give way — the Gentiles were just as Christian as their Jewish counterparts.

In his later encounters with Judaizers, Paul gives a more detailed response as to why the Jewish law is not mandatory for salvation. Gentiles are equally Christian because Jesus, as a person, is a better version of the elements that the Judaizers find appealing in Old Judaism. Since both groups have Jesus, they already have everything that the Old Testament pointed toward: "[The old practices] are a shadow of the things that were to come; the reality, however, is found in Christ" (Col. 2:17).

Christ is the Chosen One, and his people the true remnant that God has spared from the destruction of the rest: "So too, at the present time there is a remnant chosen by grace. And if by grace, then it cannot be based on works; if it were, grace would no longer be grace" (Rom. 11:5–6).

Christ is the true circumcision, the sign that God owns us: "[A] person is a Jew who is one inwardly; and circumcision is circumcision of the heart, by the Spirit, not by the written code. Such a person's praise is not from other people, but from God" (Rom. 2:29).

Christ is the true Sabbath, and we find peace when we come to him: "For if Joshua had given them rest, God would not have spoken later about another day. There remains, then, a Sabbath-rest for the people of God; for anyone who enters God's rest also rests from their works, just as God did from his" (Heb. 4:8–10).

Christ is the true guilt-offering, for which our sins are forgiven: "The blood of goats and bulls and the ashes of a heifer sprinkled on those who are ceremonially unclean sanctify them so that they are outwardly clean. How much more, then, will the blood of Christ, who through the eternal Spirit offered himself unblemished to God, cleanse our consciences from acts that lead to death, so that we may serve the living God!" (Heb. 9:13–14).

Paul also uses the Judaizing controversy to address a broader issue — the idea that we have to work hard and be a good person, whatever that might look like to us. Instead, when we trust Christ, he draws us out of sin. He has set the standards and satisfied them, so we can rest. To choose works, Paul warns, is to reject Christ altogether, not just to take Christ as a helper: "Mark my words! I, Paul, tell you that if you let yourselves be circumcised, Christ will be of no value to you at all. Again I declare to every man who lets himself be circumcised that he is obligated to keep the whole law. You who are trying to be justified by the law have been alienated from Christ; you have fallen away from grace" (Gal. 5:2–4).

Paul is quite passionate on the issue, and understandably so. Another response is found in Galatians 5:12: "As for those agitators, I wish they would go the whole way and emasculate themselves!" Paul is so perturbed that he suggests castration for those who require circumcision for others — he made his point clearly. Thus, according to the apostle and the response drafted at the Jerusalem Council in Acts 15, the Gentiles were in no way obligated to follow the restrictions of the law. They were free in Christ, who had fulfilled the demands of the law. Paul only exhorted the Gentiles to abstain from practices associated with pagan idol worship, not so that they might earn their salvation but as a response to the life-changing message of the gospel as God's free gift.

Paul's response to the teaching of the Judaizers is twofold: (1) salvation is by grace alone through faith in Christ, not by anything anyone does, and (2) Jews and Gentiles stand on equal footing before God in Christ. The law no longer serves to mark out the people of God the way it did in the past. The gospel of Jesus Christ is for the world — for everyone. The following are Bible passages in which Paul challenges the "works" model of his Judaizing opponents:

First, God saves people freely by grace (God's supernatural intervention) through faith:

- "For it is by grace you have been saved, through faith — and this is not from yourselves, it is the gift of God — not by works, so that no one can boast" (Eph. 2:8–9).
- "He has saved us and called us to a holy life — not because of anything we have done but because of his own purpose and grace. This grace was given us in Christ Jesus before the beginning of time" (2 Tim. 1:9).
- "But when the kindness and love of God our Savior appeared, he saved us, not because of righteous things we had done, but because of his mercy. He saved us through the washing of rebirth and renewal by the Holy Spirit" (Titus 3:4–5).

And second, the gospel includes both Jews and Gentiles (and anyone who believes):

- "Or is God the God of Jews only? Is he not the God of Gentiles too? Yes, of Gentiles too, since there is only one God, who will justify the circumcised by faith and the uncircumcised through that same faith" (Rom. 3:29–30).
- "Therefore, the promise comes by faith, so that it may be by grace and may be guaranteed to all Abraham's offspring — not only to those who are of the law but also to those who have the faith of Abraham. He is the father of us all" (Rom. 4:16).
- "[F]or all of you who were baptized into Christ have clothed yourselves with Christ. There is neither Jew nor Gentile, neither slave nor free, nor is there male and female, for you

are all one in Christ Jesus. If you belong to Christ, then you are Abraham's seed, and heirs according to the promise" (Gal. 3:27–29).

• "Therefore, remember that formerly you who are Gentiles by birth and called 'uncircumcised' by those who call themselves 'the circumcision' (which is done in the body by human hands) — remember that at that time you were separate from Christ, excluded from citizenship in Israel and foreigners to the covenants of the promise, without hope and without God in the world. But now in Christ Jesus you who once were far away have been brought near by the blood of Christ. For he himself is our peace, who has made the two groups one and has destroyed the barrier, the dividing wall of hostility" (Eph. 2:11–14).

Contemporary Relevance

Why does this matter today? The teaching of the Judaizers forced Paul to explain more precisely how we are saved by Jesus. God does not require us to carry out a certain command in order to restore our connection with him. Indeed, he calls us to carry out his orders as his children, servants, and creatures, but our obedience does not solve the problem of being separated from God. In fact, since obedience can become a point of pride, doing good can even be detrimental — we must sometimes repent of our virtues as well as our vices. Instead, it is the fact that God declares us to be chosen people or new creations that carries the final weight, since his word trumps all others.[7] And we are declared to be God's chosen people when we trust in Jesus, meaning that we can rest.

Grace by faith *alone*, without other qualifications, is a central reason Martin Luther took issue with the Roman Catholic Church of his day, whose stress on responding correctly to God in actions threatened to drive believers to despair. While the issue can be overemphasized to the neglect of other New Testament teachings, the grace-centeredness and inclusivity of the gospel must never be lost. This issue was about Jews and Gentiles in the first century, but the heart of the problem was something more fundamental: we tend to prioritize what *we* do (works) over what God has done (grace). For these reasons, we are tempted to exclude those who do not behave the way we behave.

Thus, while the heresy of the Judaizers was put to rest by the apostle Paul in the first century, the Judaizers' ideas still permeate the church today. The issues are no longer circumcision or ceremonial uncleanness, but the question of how the law relates to salvation is still something that many Christians remain confused about. How are our actions connected to our salvation? Paul's exhortation to the Judaizers remains as important as ever. It is not by works that we are saved but solely by the grace of Christ. In fact, to add anything to the work of Christ for salvation negates God's grace. Paul says, "I do not nullify the grace of God; for if justification were through the law, then Christ died to no purpose" (Gal. 2:21 RSV). This means that the gospel is for everyone, not just those who lived according to the rules: "the same Lord is Lord of all and richly blesses all who call on him, for, 'Everyone who calls on the name of the Lord will be saved'" (Rom. 10:12–13).

Discussion Questions

1. What does it mean for the Christian faith if Judaizing rules the day? How does Judaizing undercut the gospel?
2. In what ways can Christians still operate today like the Judaizers?
3. Do you have a pet "work" that you believe others must do (or avoid) to enjoy God's favor more fully? Maybe you wouldn't say people are saved by it — because we know that is bad theology— but perhaps at times you feel or act like their status as "good Christians" is in jeopardy because of it?
4. Who might you be excluding from the gospel? Who is the person or group of people that you just cannot imagine being

in the fold, included in the "all" of Paul's "you are *all* one in Christ Jesus" (Gal. 3:28)? How might God be challenging you to reconsider?

5. In what areas of your life have you hardened your heart to the free grace of God? Where are you under a yoke of slavery instead of finding the freedom that the love and grace of Jesus bring? In what ways have you been motivated by the grace of God?

Further Reading

Campbell, W. S. "Judaizers." In *Dictionary of Paul and His Letters*, edited by Gerald F. Hawthorne and Ralph P. Martin. Downers Grove, IL: InterVarsity, 1993.

Gathercole, Simon. "What Did Saint Paul Really Mean?" *Christianity Today* 51, no. 8 (2007), 22–28.

Rightmire, David R. "Judaizers." In *Baker Theological Dictionary of the Bible*, edited by Walter A. Elwell. Grand Rapids, MI: Baker, 1996.

Thomas R. Schreiner. *Galatians.* Zondervan Exegetical Commentary on the New Testament. Grand Rapids, MI: Zondervan, 2010.

Westerholm, Stephen. *Perspectives Old and New on Paul: The "Lutheran" Paul and His Critics.* Grand Rapids, MI: Eerdmans, 2004.

CHAPTER 2

GNOSTICS

God Hides Messages for the Enlightened

Historical Background

Gnosticism is not a specific heretical movement in church history but rather a loose collection of different religious beliefs. *Gnosis* is the Greek word for "knowledge," and Gnostics claimed to have a special knowledge that was hidden from most people. Although they often used similar terms and rituals as Christians, the Gnostics interpreted them according to deeper, secret meanings; for instance, one early text explained Jesus' claim to be the fount of living water as a metaphor for his teachings rather than for Jesus himself: "Jesus said, 'Whoever drinks from my mouth will become like me; I myself shall become that person, and the hidden things will be revealed to him.'"[1] Other characteristics that bound different Gnostic groups included the belief that matter is evil and that spirit is pure, as well as an elaborate primordial mythology.

The origins of Gnosticism are still a bit unclear. Some think Gnosticism originated as a heresy that diverged from orthodox Christian teaching, while others see the movement as an independent, non-Christian movement stemming from either paganism or Judaism. For example, church historian Everett Ferguson argues that "Gnosticism seems to have grown up concurrently with

Christianity in a similar environment (but from different roots), with the two having some interactions in the first century before Gnosticism developed into a separate religion in the second century."[2] That Gnosticism had contact with early Christianity is almost certain — there seem to be anti-Gnostic warnings in the letters of Paul (although many Gnostics also liked to claim Paul for themselves), as well as 1 John. However, the first certain identification comes from the mid-second century, in the writings of Irenaeus of Lyons. His book *Against Heresies* provides detailed descriptions and refutations of a number of different Gnostic sects, including Valentinians, Ophites, Sethians, Cainites, and the followers of Basilides. Based on the number of sects and the wide range of beliefs, we can certainly conclude that the Gnostics had been established for some time before Irenaeus wrote.

Irenaeus's work was a staple for later scholars of heresy, and it represented much of the information on Gnosticism that was available for some time. Since Irenaeus and his disciples were obviously hostile toward the Gnostics, researchers didn't believe that they were representing Gnostic beliefs fairly. However, the relatively recent discovery of a library of Gnostic texts near Nag Hammadi in Egypt (containing forty new documents from the late fourth century) has greatly increased scholars' ability to analyze and describe early forms of Gnosticism. The library contains the sacred scriptures of many of the groups that Irenaeus wrote about, and although it confirms most of Irenaeus's information, it also provides a more detailed glimpse into their world.

Heretical Teaching

Definition

The Gnostics differed widely in their beliefs, and some scholars have wondered if it is appropriate to use a single term to denote all of them. Nevertheless, Birger Pearson has provided a list of several categories that broadly describe Gnosticism:[3]

Gnosis: The adherents of Gnosticism regarded *gnosis* (secret knowledge), rather than faith in Christ or observance of the law, as the way of salvation. The saving "knowledge" involved a revelation of the true nature both of the self and of God. For Gnostics, self-knowledge *is* knowledge of God.

Theology: The Gnostics often believed in one, transcendent, supreme god who was utterly silent. This god was revealed by the coming of Jesus (as opposed to God's interactions with the Hebrews). However, there are numerous intermediate gods (known as Aeons) and dark, evil gods (known as Archons) that hover just above the earth.

Cosmology: The universe, having been created by an inferior and ignorant power, is a dark prison in which human souls are held captive.

Anthropology: A human being is a divine spark that originated in the transcendent divine world and, by means of gnosis, can be released from the cosmic prison and return to its heavenly origin. The human body, on the other hand, is part of the cosmic prison from which the spirit (the "real" person) must be redeemed.

Experimental: Mystical experience was an important part of Gnosticism. Religious experience, for the Gnostics, involved joy in the salvation won by gnosis, as well as an extreme alienation from, and revolt against, the physical world.

Myth: What held everything together for Gnostics is myth. One of the most characteristic features of Gnosticism was its impulse to create an elaborate mythical system. Each Gnostic teacher created new elements to be added to their received myth, and, with such elaborations, Gnostic myths could become more and more complicated as they developed.

Parasitical: What makes Gnosticism so hard to define is, finally, its parasitical character. It borrowed freely from other religions, and its members sometimes attached themselves to other congregations.

Beliefs

Gnostic myth is best understood by thinking of a pyramid. At the top is the supreme transcendent god, who lives in "silent silence."[4] There is usually a divine mother who follows, and from the two of them there are hordes of Aeons, or lesser gods. Following the Aeons down the pyramid, the gods become more numerous, but also less good and less powerful. Finally, at the bottom of the pyramid are Archons, or evil gods. The Archons are less powerful and less good than humankind, but they have managed to hold sway over humankind by their terrible illusions. (Think of the manipulative deceptions of the Wizard of Oz.)

The God of the Hebrew Bible is considered one such Archon. In the Gnostic myth *On the Origin of the World*, the arrogant, evil creator god Yaldabaoth is meant to be identified with the God of Israel: "He boasted over and over again and said to [the wise gods], 'I don't need anything.... I am God, and there is no other but me.'"[5] Yaldabaoth is crude and petty, and he fears the enlightenment of humankind, for it was prophesied to him that he would be overshadowed when humans reached their full potential: "The human will trample upon you as potter's clay is trampled, and you will descend with those who are yours to your mother the abyss."[6] Consequently, it is in God's interest to keep humans fearful and ignorant. In some versions, Satan is a hero who freed humans from this arrogant creator god by pointing them to the fruit of knowledge (or *gnosis*).[7] Sects who held this view included the Sethians, Ophites, and Barbeliotes.

The role of Jesus in these myths is to dispel the errors of the old pagan religions (as well as Judaism), along with the fearful illusions of the Archons. Since matter is evil, Jesus did not come in the flesh or suffer. Instead, Jesus was pure spirit, and he merely mimicked the appearance of a man in order to show how flimsy the material prison really is. A typical interpretation of how a pure-spirit Jesus redeems the world appears in *The Second Discourse of the Great Seth*, where Jesus himself describes to the Gnostics what really happened at the crucifixion. "[The children of the petty gods] saw me and punished me, but someone else, their father, drank the gall and the vinegar; it was not I. They were striking me with a scourge, but someone else, Simon, bore the cross on his shoulder. Someone else wore the crown of thorns. And I was on high, poking fun at all the excesses of the ruler and the fruit of their error and conceit. I was laughing at their ignorance."[8]

The Gnostics too could laugh with this Jesus at the error of those who worshiped the God of Israel, since they believed their eyes had been opened to the true nature of things. Because they thought Jesus was an example rather than a savior, the Gnostics could become enlightened with him.

In other versions of this Gnostic myth, Jesus' primary task is less to combat Archons than to reveal the silent transcendent god and awaken people to their identity as gods. *The Gospel of Truth*, for instance, talks of how God the Father had a book that would reveal the true nature of the world, but no one could read it without dying. Jesus, in an act of heroism, underwent that task on the cross, which released the power that was concealed in the book:

> Jesus appeared,
> put on that book,
> was nailed to a tree
> and published the Father's edict on the cross.
> Oh, what a great teaching![9]

Although this might seem like a poetic version of Christian teachings on the crucifixion, the key to salvation here is knowledge, rather than divine intervention. When Jesus was crucified, people not only knew the thoughts of the previously unseen Father but also realized that they were gods themselves: "He found them within himself, and they found him within themselves."[10]

Gnosticism certainly borrowed the theme of redemption from Christianity, but the means of redemption in Gnostic thought was not Christ's work. The Gnostics were quite clear that the orthodox interpretation of the cross had no place in their writings; a gospel purportedly written by some of Jesus' disciples records, "When [Jesus] saw us happy, he said, 'Woe to you who are in need of an advocate / Woe to you who stand in need of grace / Blessed will they be who have spoken out and acquired grace for themselves.'"[11] Instead, believers were responsible for forging their own spiritual paths, as historian Henry Chadwick notes: "The content of the Gnostic gospel was an attempt to rouse the soul from its sleep-walking condition and to make it aware of the high destiny to which it is called."[12] In contrast to the New Testament Gospels, Gnostic texts deemphasized the idea of a historical redeemer and instead focused on supposedly deep and cryptic sayings of Jesus.

Ethics

As with beliefs (of which the above are only a small sampling), it is difficult to discuss a system of ethics, ritual, or daily life that applied to *all* Gnostics. Some writings, usually those that more closely resembled the Christian gospels that they mimicked, urged good works and care for one another. However, these writings seem to be the exception rather than the rule. Their confidence that they had "seen through" the normal ways of the world, coupled with the belief that matter is evil and will not be redeemed, led many Gnostics to live with extreme self-indulgence, especially in regard to food and sex. In his book on Gnostic ethics, Edwin Yamauchi comments, "The followers of Carpocrates [a Gnostic teacher] ... taught that promiscuity was God's law ... [but] it should be noted that though the antinomian Gnostics indulged in sexual license, they did not want to engender any children."[13] In other words, food and sex became purely means of pleasure rather than tools.

Other Gnostics, such as the Encratites, drew the opposite conclusion from the doctrine that matter is evil. They practiced extreme asceticism; instead of pampering their bodies, they starved and beat them, determined to kill the evil matter that had enslaved them and to set their divine spirits free. Examples of this attitude appear in the *Acts of Judas Thomas*, in which abstinence from sex is promoted as the way to heaven.

Many of these trends had appeared in the church as early as the letters of the apostle Paul to the churches at Corinth and Colossae. The spiritual elite at Corinth questioned the resurrection and believed the body to be meaningless, which had profound moral consequences — such as the promiscuous sexual behavior mentioned earlier. Moreover, at Colossae the believers observed special ascetic practices and worshiped intermediate angelic powers. Because of these similarities, some scholars think that the congregations at Corinth and Colossae were influenced by early strands of Gnostic thought.

Orthodox Response

Although small in number, the Gnostics and their teachings wreaked havoc in the mainstream Christian community. Their use of Scripture and Christian language meant that they could attend Christian services seemingly as one of the faithful. Their idea of an elite, informed clique was naturally appealing, as was their dismissal of the Hebrew Bible with its stories of anger and war and vengeance. Being Gnostic was associated with being urbane, sophisticated, and intelligent, which was a powerful draw at a time when ordinary Christians had few intellectual centers.

To the churches at Corinth and Colossae, Paul battled the Gnostic heresy with a robust Christology — teaching about the person and work of Christ. His solution to their abhorrent views of the body, the resurrection, and salvation was to point them to the supremacy of Christ in his incarnation, life, death, and victorious resurrection.

After the time of the apostles, Christian leaders responded to Gnosticism in two ways. The first was to try to identify and exclude Gnostic teachers and Gnostic writings from their ranks. The first canons (lists of books recognized as authoritative Scripture) were

formed in the mid-second century as part of a reaction to a teacher
of a different heresy named Marcion (discussed in detail later), who
had tried to create his own Bible, excluding the Old Testament and
much of the New. In response to Marcion, lists were drawn up of
"the books we have used from the beginning" as Scripture, such as
the Muratorian Canon. It is perhaps no coincidence that the forma-
tion of the first canons corresponds with the composition of most of
the major Gnostic works. The Christian canon attempted to preserve
the authentic biblical writings of the apostles so that churches would
be wary of the new, spurious works that were beginning to circulate.

However, it was not enough simply to circle the wagons and try
to keep the Gnostics out. Irenaeus of Lyons and other intellectuals
such as Hippolytus, Epiphanius, and Tertullian worked to mount
an effective Christian response to Gnosticism. Irenaeus urged the
Gnostics to repent of the spiritual pride that was the heart of their
religion: "It is ... better and more profitable to belong to the simple
and unlettered class, and by means of love to attain to nearness to
God."[14] God was not trying to trick people or hide himself from the
unsophisticated, said Irenaeus, but rather desired the salvation of
all people. Thus, the Old Testament demonstrated the workings of
God in simple, physical terms that everyone could understand, and
it prophesied the coming of God in the flesh to fulfill that salvation. When Jesus came, he confirmed the Old Testament both by
fulfilling the prophecies and by relying on specific images from the
Hebrew Scriptures: "He declares: For in this place is One greater
than the temple. But [the words] greater and less are not applied to
those things which have nothing in common between themselves."[15]
In other words, Irenaeus said, Christ was superseding the Old Covenant, but he was not opposing it, and when he spoke of his Father
in heaven he did not mean a new supreme god but was reaffirming
the lordship of the God of Israel. Finally, Irenaeus pointed out that
Christ was resurrected in the flesh, not as a spirit, and that this had
enormous implications for the future. The Gnostic objection to the
body had truth to it, he acknowledged — the flesh was weak and sick

and seemingly useless. But God's power was great enough to transform it into something new, not simply to discard it.[16]

Irenaeus's approach proved immensely popular and eventually overshadowed a second response from other Christians, which was to try to reclaim the word "Gnostic" for orthodox Christian use. Clement of Alexandria, a third-century theologian, expounded the duties of a Christian Gnostic in his work *Miscellanies*. According to him, a Gnostic was one who had special spiritual insight and communion with God, but instead of using that knowledge to feel superior to the mundane Christians around him, the real Gnostic helped them to know God better: "The Gnostic, then, is pious, [if he] cares first for himself, then for his neighbours, that they may become very good."[17] It was a role for someone who had time, education, and piety to strengthen brothers and sisters who could not spare the time for advanced study. The idea of a "Christian Gnostic" endured until the late fourth century, but finally fell into disrepute.

Contemporary Relevance

The discovery of the Nag Hammadi scrolls has given weight to a perception that Jesus' teachings were hijacked by an institutionalized, patriarchal church in the fourth century, because it seems as though there is secret information about Jesus that mainstream Christianity has been withholding. Dan Brown's bestselling novel *The Da Vinci Code*, to cite only one example, appeals to information from the Gnostic gospels as factual truth. The character Sir Leigh Teabing, an expert on early Christianity, describes the suppression of the Gnostics by the church: "More than *eighty* gospels were considered for the New Testament, and yet only a relative few were chosen for inclusion."[18] Teabing then blunders, however, when he says, "The early Church needed to convince the world that the mortal prophet Jesus was a *divine* being. Therefore, any gospels that described *earthly* aspects of Jesus' life had to be omitted from the Bible."[19] Ironically, the problem with the Gnostics was exactly the opposite — the church had to fight to show that Jesus was human and material against groups that would accept only his divinity.

Gnosticism has made a surprising spiritual renaissance. Gnostic churches have been established[20] and writings about Gnosticism are currently in vogue in bookstores. Although the strong asceticism that characterized some early forms of Gnosticism is almost entirely lacking today, Gnosticism has also contributed to New Age spirituality. Consider the promise of a book featured on Oprah in recent years called *The Secret*: "Without The Power you would not have been born. Without The Power, there wouldn't be a single human being on the planet. Every discovery, invention, and human creation comes from The Power. Perfect health, incredible relationships, a career you love, a life filled with happiness, and the money you need to be, do, and have everything you want, *all* come from The Power."[21]

"The Power" is classic Gnosticism — a silent, supreme god that also lives inside of you and who will allow you to become as powerful as you wish. Often, as in Gnosticism, a Jesus separate from the God of Israel is featured in New Age beliefs as a spirit guide or key to enlightenment, but never as a Lord who calls for repentance and dependence on the Savior's life, death, and resurrection.[22]

What sets Christianity apart from Gnosticism is that in Christ, the supreme character of the once-hidden God has now been definitively and exhaustively revealed, so much so that Jesus could tell his followers that those who had seen him had seen his Father. There is no God that remains hidden from plain sight or reserved for an elite, enlightened group of people. Instead, Christ has made supreme knowledge of God available in his life, death, and resurrection, and that knowledge was written and recounted in the Christian Scriptures that testify to Christ.

Paul writes in 2 Corinthians 4:4–6 that the message of Christ, not ourselves, is supreme: "The god of this age has blinded the minds of unbelievers, so that they cannot see the light of the gospel that displays the glory of Christ, who is the image of God. For what we preach is not ourselves, but Jesus Christ as Lord, and ourselves as your servants for Jesus' sake. For God, who said, 'Let light shine out of darkness,' made his light shine in our hearts to give us the light of the knowledge of God's glory displayed in the face of Christ."

Discussion Questions

1. What do you make of the idea of a silent god? How does that compare with the God of the Bible?
2. How does the resurrection affect how we view our bodies?
3. The Gnostic creed was "Knowledge is power." Is that true at all? Is knowledge an important part of being a Christian?
4. How does Christian knowledge relate to Christian practice? Is it possible, according to Scripture, to have knowledge of God without also allowing that knowledge to affect one's behavior?

Further Reading

Clement of Alexandria. *Miscellanies* VII. *http://www.earlychristianwritings .com/text/clement-stromata-book7.html*.

Ferguson, Everett. *Backgrounds of Early Christianity*. 2nd ed. Grand Rapids, MI: Eerdmans, 1993.

Irenaeus of Lyons. *Against Heresies*. *http://www.newadvent.org/ fathers/0103.htm*.

Meyer, Marvin, ed. *The Nag Hammadi Scriptures*. New York: Harper-Collins, 2007.

Pagels, Elaine. *The Gnostic Paul: Gnostic Exegesis of the Pauline Letters*. Philadelphia: Trinity Press International, 1975.

Smith, Carl B. II, *No Longer Jews: The Search for Gnostic Origins*. Peabody, MA: Hendrickson, 2004.

CHAPTER 3

MARCION

Vengeful Yahweh versus Gentle Jesus

Historical Background

Marcion (ca. 85–160) was the son of a Christian bishop and a teacher in Rome. Although unbiased historical information is scant,[1] we know that Marcion was a wealthy ship owner from Sinope in Pontus, with excellent organizational skills. Around AD 140 he arrived at Rome, where he was welcomed by the church and soon donated large amounts of money and a building. But by AD 144, Marcion's views had gotten him into trouble, and he was excommunicated from the church.

Marcion's trouble began when he became involved with Cerdo, an early Gnostic teacher (see chapter 2).[2] Cerdo influenced Marcion's thought toward dualism, a worldview that pits two basic realities against each other. Gnostics were known for teaching a spirit/flesh dualism, in which spirit is good and flesh is evil — an idea contrary to the Bible. Marcion did not exactly adopt Gnosticism, but he was intrigued by the concept of dualism and applied it to the Old and New Testaments. According to Marcion, the God of the Old Testament was a wrathful, vengeful deity who wanted to keep humankind subject to himself, while Christ was sent by the real supreme God to reintroduce the old religion of love and peace.

The massive amount of literature written against Marcion over the years by numerous theologians indicate that this man was no small-time fringe teacher but a major threat to orthodoxy. In fact, church historian Henry Chadwick calls Marcion "the most radical and to the church the most formidable of heretics."[3] W. H. C. Frend, a British historian, comments, "For nearly a century after his death (c. 160), [Marcion] was the arch-heretic, condemned in turn by individuals who were vastly different in outlook: Polycarp, Justin, Irenaeus, Clement, Tertullian, Hippolytus, the Latin writer known as Pseudo-Tertullian, Bardesanes, and Origen. He was distinguished in his age."[4] Distinguished, but not in a flattering way. Irenaeus recalled a meeting between Bishop Polycarp and Marcion, during which Marcion asked Polycarp if he remembered him. Polycarp replied, "I do know you, the first-born of Satan."[5]

After he was no longer welcome in Rome, Marcion put his organizational skills to work traveling and establishing new alternative churches sympathetic to his view. Eventually his influence stretched all around the Mediterranean, and it lasted for a couple of centuries until the first Christian emperors suppressed Marcionism.

Heretical Teaching

Behind Marcion's practical influence of money and political connections lay a theology founded on extreme dualism. This can be seen in his most well-known book, *Antithesis*, in which he pitted the New Testament against the Old Testament:

Marcion saw too many discrepancies between the Testaments. Old Testament passages suggest there are things God does not know, whereas the New Testament teaches that Jesus knows everything. The problems that Marcion wrestled with are similar to the problems that modern readers often experience. Why does God need to ask questions, if he's all-knowing? Why does the Old Testament attribute to God qualities that we might consider petty — anger and jealousy and being arbitrary? The solution to this dilemma seemed

OLD TESTAMENT	NEW TESTAMENT
"And the Lord Yahweh called unto Adam, and said unto him, 'Where art thou?'" (Gen. 3:9).	"But when Jesus perceived their thoughts, He answering said unto them, 'Why do you reason in your hearts?'" (Luke 5:22).
"And Elijah answered and said to the captain of fifty, 'If I be a man of God, then let fire come down from heaven, and consume thee and thy fifty.' And there came down fire from heaven, and consumed him and his fifty" (2 Kings 1:9–10).	[Jesus' disciples]: "'Lord, wilt Thou that we command fire to come down from heaven, and consume them, even as Elijah did?' But He turned and rebuked them, and said, 'Ye know not what manner of spirit ye are of; for the Son of man is not come to destroy men's lives, but to save them'" (Luke 9:54–55).
"I form light, and create darkness: I make peace, and create evil: I the Lord Yahweh do all these things" (Isa. 45:7).	"God is light, and in Him is no darkness at all" (1 John 1:5b). "God is love" (1 John 4:16).
"I the Lord your God am a jealous God" (Exod. 20:5). "[F]or the Lord, Whose name is Jealous, is a jealous God" (Exod. 34:14).[6]	"Love knows no jealousy" (1 Cor. 13:4).

See "Antithesis" at *http://www.earlychristianwritings.com/marcion.html.*

clear to Marcion. There was not one God but two — the Yahweh of the Old Testament and Jesus of the New Testament — both bitter enemies, and by coming to Israel, Jesus was challenging the rule of Yahweh. Marcion taught that Jesus Christ was sent by an unknown Father to save us from Yahweh's evil wrath. Unlike many early heretics, Marcion was attentive to the Old Testament, particularly Isaiah

39–66. In 45:7 he found, "I form the light and create darkness, I bring prosperity and create disaster; I, [Yahweh], do all these things." Interpreting this passage in a narrow, literal way led Marcion to conclude that Yahweh is the one who causes the darkness and evil in the world rather than testifying that he is the supreme God. Marcion dubbed the cruel God of the Old Testament "Yahweh" and the kind father of the New Testament "Abba."

Because of his highly negative view of Yahweh, Marcion became radically anti-Jewish, rejecting Christianity's early struggle with Judaism for the right to be the true Israel.[6] He found the church's desire to be identified as the true Israel misguided. In his eyes, he was attempting to liberate the church from captivity to the law, and he believed that the only way to do this was to rid Christianity of all traces of Judaism. Tertullian summarized it best: "Marcion's special and principal work is the separation of the law and the gospel."[7] Marcion wanted nothing to do with the Old Testament law. Because the content written by the author of the law was so different from the content written by the author of the gospel, Marcion believed that the two authors could not be the same; the God who gave the law could not be the God who gave the gospel.

To solidify the wedge between the law and gospel, Marcion created his own canon, or list of sacred books he thought genuine. He rejected all allegorical interpretations of Scripture, which were often used to make difficult sections more palatable; only a literal approach of reading Scripture at face value could be acceptable for it to be authoritative. Marcion selected books from the New Testament that he believed to be faithful to his guideline of separating the law and the gospel. He cut out the Old Testament altogether. He argued that the Old Testament was tied up in the law, and that faith had superseded it in the gracious new era Christ ushered in. Therefore it was obsolete. Even several New Testament books were not safe from Marcion's canonical knife. All references to Jesus' Jewishness were removed, along with anything that he felt had been "corrupted" by Judaizing elements. The only books to survive the cut in Marcion's

Bible were a mutilated version of the gospel of Luke and ten of Paul's epistles.[8] He idolized Paul as the great enemy of the law. With this new Bible completely free from law, Marcion's version of the gospel emphasized spirituality, faith, and grace. This unknown Father Jesus revealed was kind, forgiving, and gracious, unlike the known Yahweh, who was angry, vengeful, and just.

In addition to his assault on the Christian Scriptures, Marcion's heretical teachings include a destruction of the humanity of Christ. Because Marcion interpreted Christianity through a dualistic worldview, which saw all created things as evil, he wanted to dismiss anything from the Bible that was concerned with the earthly realm.[9] Notably, because of his disdain for the material world, Marcion was skeptical that any divine redeemer could be born of a woman. For this reason, he rejected Jesus' birth story, and, as church historian Stephen Nichols puts it, "His Jesus floats down out of the sky at the wedding at Capernaum. (No wonder they ran out of wine)."[10] Christ's humanity was denied, so therefore salvation was only for the soul.

Orthodox Response

The massive volume of antiheretical literature directed against the Marcionite heresy is a testimony to the heresy's importance. Marcion's rejection of Jesus' humanity caused the church to develop a complete defense of the doctrine. To this end, Tertullian, a leader of the church in North Africa, in AD 207–8 led the charge in his work *Against Marcion*, which was composed of five books that spelled out Marcion's ideas before countering them with argument after argument. Tertullian saw Marcion's denial of Christ's humanity as detrimental to Christianity, because, "The sufferings of Christ will be found not to warrant faith in him. For he suffered nothing who did not truly suffer; and a phantom could not truly suffer. God's entire work therefore is subverted. Christ's death, wherein lies the whole weight and fruit of the Christian name, is denied."[11]

Tertullian also questioned Marcion's authority because he had no connection to the earliest Christians; he demanded of Marcion that he produce one Marcionite church that could trace its descent from an apostle. With no connection to the apostolic tradition, Marcion was to be treated like a trespasser when he talked about Scripture. Tertullian challenged him: "Who are you? When and whence do you come?... What are you doing on my land? By what right are you cutting down my timber, Marcion?... This property belongs to me ... I am heir to the apostles."[12]

Since both the Old and New Testaments testify to the nature and work of God, Tertullian rejected dualism and argued there is only one God. God is the supreme being, subordinate to no one. He declared, "Christian verity has distinctly declared this principle, 'God is not, if He is not one.'"[13] If there were any being equal to God, God would no longer be the supreme being, and thereby would no longer be worthy of worship.

Tertullian also argued for the goodness of the material creation, which displays God's wisdom and glory, and demonstrated the futility of condemning it: "Marcion has ridiculed the insects but he cannot imitate the skills of bee, ant, spider, silkworm or any other of God's tiny creatures."[14] Tertullian points out the hypocrisy of Marcion's followers for their shameless "addiction to astrology." Are not the stars part of Yahweh's creation they depreciate? Contrary to Marcion's assertion, nature points to the goodness of God and was created as a good thing before sin came into the world.

Against Marcion's dualism between justice and love, Tertullian argued that God is both good and just. Without justice God "would have to give commands without intentions to execute them and forbid sins without intentions of punishing them."[15] Tertullian reasoned, "He takes no offense, therefore his will is not wronged." If this is the case, he challenged Marcion, why not live a life dedicated to selfish pleasure? But by the fact that Marcion did live as though there is a right and a wrong, he showed that God does carry out his promises of punishment for sin.[16] Tertullian reached to the heart of the matter in salvation. If there is no retribution for doing what is forbidden, how could God deliver us from sin and death when we were never handed over to sin and death in the first place? Justice is better seen as an agent of goodness than as the enemy of goodness.

Finally, Tertullian set out to prove that Christ belongs to the Creator rather than opposing him.[17] Marcion's problem, Tertullian suggested, was that "Marcion used the knife, not the pen, massacring scripture to suit his own material."[18] Even with Marcion's mutilated version of the gospel of Luke, one can see that Christ "has administered (the Creator's) dispensations, fulfilled his prophecies, promoted his laws, given reality to his promises, revived his mighty power, remolded his determinations, expressed his attributes, his properties."[19] The overwhelming conclusion was that Marcion's division between law and gospel, Old and New Testaments, and flesh and spirit was foreign to the truth.

Irenaeus also spoke forcefully against Marcion, saying that "he mutilated the Gospel according to Luke, removing all the narratives of the Lord's birth, and also removing much of the teaching of the discourses of the Lord wherein he is most manifestly described as acknowledging the maker of this universe to be his father. Thus he persuaded his disciples that he himself was more trustworthy than the apostles, who handed down the Gospel; though he gave to them not a Gospel but a fragment of a Gospel."[20] Furthermore, Irenaeus writes, Marcion "says that salvation will be of our souls only, of those souls which have learned his teaching; the body, because forsooth it is taken from the earth, cannot partake in salvation."[21]

While Marcion was excommunicated from the church in Rome in 144, because he was a wealthy man he was able to establish a significant following throughout the next several centuries. However, the struggle also provided an opportunity for the church to clarify several major doctrines. For one thing, Marcion and his "New Testament" — the first to be compiled — forced the church to recognize a core canon of New Testament Scripture books: the four gospels and the letters of Paul. The Old Testament was also reaffirmed as Christian Scripture; Tertullian declared the Hebrew Bible is indeed the Word of God, arguing in *Against Marcion* that the two Testaments of the Bible are not contrary.[22] At the same time, the church affirmed that the New Testament books are to be considered as fully authoritative as God's revelation in the Hebrew Bible.

Contemporary Relevance

Marcion is relevant to the church today because much contemporary teaching about Jesus and the Bible merely restates Marcion's claims about the struggle between a God of love and a God of justice. Richard Dawkins, in his *New York Times* bestseller *The God Delusion*, writes, "The God of the Old Testament is arguably the most unpleasant character in all fiction: jealous and proud of it; a petty, unjust, unforgiving control-freak; a vindictive, bloodthirsty ethnic cleanser; a misogynistic, homophobic, racist, infanticidal, genocidal, filicidal, pestilential, megalomaniacal, sadomasochistic, capriciously malevolent bully."[23] This view is quite similar to Marcion's and still wreaks havoc in the church today.

A conclusion from church historian Bruce Shelley could not be stated better: "By retaining the Old Testament the church scored two important points. First, it insisted that faith for the Christian would have to reconcile both the wrath and love of God. Marcion's message was too easy. By eliminating the Old Testament he hoped to make the love of God central for the Christian. But love that never faces the demands of justice is not Christian love. It was not the love Marcion's hero knew! Paul found in the Cross not only a demonstration of God's love but a display of his righteousness. Christ's death, he said, allowed God to be both just and the justifier of all who believe in Jesus (Rom. 3:25, 26). That is the marvel of the grace of God Marcion missed."[24]

Second, by retaining the Old Testament, the church underscored the importance of history for the Christian faith. Christianity is a historical religion not just in the sense that it comes from the past or that it is associated with a historical character named Jesus. It is historical because it stems from the belief that within history itself, in a particular place, at a particular time, God himself played a role in human affairs. Historian Philip Schaff remarked that in Marcion's view it is "as if God had neglected the world for thousands of years until he suddenly appeared in Christ."[25]

As Tertullian rightly declared, if Christ was not truly human, then he could not truly suffer, and if he did not truly suffer, then he cannot be the one who has identified with us as fallen human beings, winning our salvation in his atoning death and life-giving resurrection.

Discussion Questions

1. Why is it an oversimplification to say that the Old Testament is about justice with no grace and the New Testament is about grace with no justice?
2. What would be lost if the church disregards the Old Testament?
3. Consider Romans 11:11–24. Marcion wanted to rid the church of anything that had to do with Israel. Is that what Paul wants as well? How should we think about ethnically Jewish people (not the geopolitical nation or Judaism) in light of this passage?

Further Reading

Foster, Paul. "Marcion: His Life, Works, Beliefs, and Impact." *Expository Times* 121 (2010): 269–80.

Marcion. "Antithesis: Marcion and Contradictions between the Old Testament God and the New Testament." *Http://gnosis.org/library/marcion/antithes.htm*. (Note: *Antithesis* is a reconstruction of Marcion's lost work by the same name. The link begins with a modern commentary that explains Marcion's reasoning on his own terms.)

Moll, Sebastian. *The Arch-Heretic Marcion.* Wissenschaftliche Unter-
    suchungen zum Neuen Testament 250. Tubingen: Mohr Siebeck,
    2010.
Osborn, Eric. *Tertullian, First Theologian of the West.* New York: Cam-
    bridge Univ. Press, 1997.

CHAPTER 4

DOCETISTS

The Spiritual Is Good, the Physical Is Evil

Historical Background

For many people today, it seems natural to believe that Jesus Christ was a human and a struggle to believe that he was God. A few Christian offshoots also struggled with this problem. For instance, a Jewish sect called Ebionitism began to flourish in the early centuries of the Christian era. They regarded Jesus merely as an ordinary human being — the biological son of Mary and Joseph and not the Son of God. However, most philosophers of the first few centuries had the opposite problem — they struggled to understand how Jesus could possibly be human. The reason that Christ's humanity was such a puzzle was not because people considered the gospel to be legend or mythology but because it seemed impossible that anything good, spiritual, pure, and divine should mix with anything evil, ugly, filthy, and decaying.

The apostle Paul declared to the church in Corinth, "Jews demand signs and Greeks look for wisdom, but we preach Christ crucified: a stumbling block to Jews and foolishness to Gentiles" (1 Cor. 1:22–23). A man's death on the cross was unanimously seen as shameful and degrading. To those outside the church, there was nothing heroic or inspiring about such a death. It was the pinnacle of unsightliness and therefore the opposite of the spiritual, which was supposed to be obviously good and beautiful. Therefore, a movement sprang up in certain intellectual circles to redefine Jesus in purely spiritual terms.

Heretical Teaching

Docetism, which derives from the Greek verb "to seem" or "appear," taught that Jesus Christ was totally divine and that his humanity was merely an appearance. Although he seemed to have a human body, he was not subject to any kind of human experiences. This included being immune to human "birth, fatigue, thirst, hunger, suffering, [and] death."[1]

Unlike many other heresies, Docetism was not linked to a particular leader or representative. It should be viewed as more of a tendency among some in theology. Usually proponents of Gnosticism (see chapter 2) or Marcionism (see chapter 3) were associated with Docetism, but it was not limited to these groups.

Docetism developed to make Christianity more acceptable to pagan societies. Many societies, especially those influenced by Greek or Persian dualistic thought, viewed flesh as evil. The very thought of God incarnating as a man was unthinkable. The incarnation inevitably implied suffering. As a man, Jesus Christ was subjected to the humiliation of being a helpless baby. He required food and drink to survive. When he was fasting in the wilderness for forty days, he was tempted. He was spat upon, beaten, and crucified. All these events were thought to be beneath a great and spiritual God who transcends everything.

The apocryphal (that is, of dubious authority) *Gospel of Peter* illustrates a Docetic view of Christ's sufferings. It says that during his crucifixion, Jesus "kept silence, as one feeling no pain,"[2] which implied "that His bodily make-up was illusory."[3] The Docetic idea that God must be free from suffering and impure matter can also be seen in the words put into the mouth of Christ by a Gnostic: "But

I was not afflicted at all. Those who were there punished me. And I did not die in reality but in appearance, lest I be put to *shame* by them because these were my kinsfolk. I removed the *shame* from me and I did not become fainthearted in the face of what happened to me at their hands. I was about to succumb to fear, and I suffered according to their sight and thought, in order that they may never find any word to speak about them. For my death which they think happened, (happened) to them in their error and blindness, since they nailed their man unto their death. For their (thoughts) did not see me, for they were deaf and blind."[4]

The writer goes on to explain that the executioners mistakenly crucified Simon of Cyrene, who helped carry the cross. "Meanwhile, the triumphant Christ invisibly present behind the scene, was 'laughing at their ignorance.'"[5] For the Redeemer to be effective, in the minds of Docetic theologians, everything about the earthly ministry of Christ had to be retold to free Christ from the weakness of flesh and matter.

Orthodox Response

Ignatius of Antioch (ca. 50–117) was one of the earliest to defend orthodoxy against Docetism. History remembers him as a disciple of the apostle John and one of the five apostolic fathers, the next generation of leaders after the apostles died. Docetism prompted Ignatius to formulate one of the earliest, albeit informal, Christian creeds: "Be deaf, therefore, when any would speak to you apart from (at variance with) Jesus Christ [the Son of God], who was descended from the family of David, born of Mary, who truly was born [both of God and of the Virgin ... truly took a body; for the Word became flesh and dwelt among us without sin ...], ate and drank [truly], truly suffered persecution under Pontius Pilate, was truly [and not in appearance] crucified and died ... who was also truly raised from the dead [and rose after three days], his Father raising him up ... [and after having spent forty days with the Apostles, was received up to the Father, and sits on his right hand, waiting till his enemies are put under his feet]."[6]

Notice the emphatic repetition of the word "truly." And also notice the outright statement that Christ's crucifixion was "not in appearance."

At the end of his life, Ignatius was sentenced to suffer the fate of a martyr, which he gladly accepted. He dissuaded fellow Christians from protecting him, because he wanted truly to experience death and truly to rise from the dead like his Savior. Otherwise, he argued, "If the Lord were in the body in appearance only, and were crucified in appearance only, then am I also bound in appearance only." Then he rhetorically asks, "And why have I also surrendered myself to death, to fire, to the sword, to the wild beasts? But [in fact,] I endure all things for Christ, not in appearance only, but in reality, that I may suffer together with Him."[7] In Ignatius's eyes, it would have been ridiculous for him to have been imprisoned for proclaiming one who merely appeared to suffer for his sake. Indeed, it would make no sense for martyrs to die for an illusion. Salvation depends on Christ's really being a man who suffered and was resurrected, so that those in Christ may die and rise with him.

Polycarp of Smyrna (69–155), another apostolic father and a fellow disciple of the apostle John, took a different approach from his friend Ignatius. While Ignatius described positively what we should believe and then warned readers to avoid Docetism, Polycarp cursed Docetism.

He began by quoting his mentor, John: "For whosoever does not confess that Jesus Christ has come in the flesh, is an antichrist" (1 John 4:3). He continued, "And whosoever does not confess his suffering on the cross, is of the devil; and whosoever … says that there is neither a resurrection nor a judgment, he is the first-born of Satan."[8] Strong words, but he concludes with the hope that Jesus Christ "bore our sins in His own body on the tree" and "endured all things for us, that we might live in him."[9] In other words, only a real death on the cross can enable Christ to bear our sins so that we might live. The docetic alternative would have been a sham.

Irenaeus (ca. 130–202), a disciple of Polycarp, wrote an important — and surprisingly amusing — five-volume work titled *Against Heresies* to refute Gnosticism, taking special aim at one of Docetism's prominent teachers, Valentinus (ca. 136–165). Irenaeus's unique contribution to theology was making the incarnation the centerpiece of God's plan, arguing that the incarnation is utterly necessary for salvation.[10]

Docetics thought of Christ's work as purely spiritual, and therefore the incarnation was not necessary to salvation. Irenaeus turned this argument on its head by saying that the incarnation itself was redemptive. Using Paul's argument from Romans 5, Irenaeus argued that Christ's human body is the spearhead of a movement to transform creation as the second Adam. The first Adam sinned at the fall and therefore as the "head" he plunged the world into sin. Christ had to be made of the same substance Adam was made of in order to restore the world as the "new head."[11] Irenaeus rightly taught that redemption was not an escape from creation but a process of restoring creation.

Contemporary Relevance

As Stephen Nichols points out, much contemporary popular theology tends to "view Jesus as sort of floating six inches off the ground as he walked upon the earth"[12] or attributes to him a glowing angelic radiance. These expressions of theology tend toward the heresy of Docetism and, more important, do not match the biblical picture of Jesus given to us in the Gospels. While on earth, Jesus experienced hunger (Matt. 4:2) and thirst (John 19:28), showed compassion (Matt. 9:36), was tired (John 4:6), felt sorrow to the point of weeping (John 11:35), and grew in wisdom (Luke 2:52). Yet in all of his humanness, Jesus never sinned (Heb. 4:15).

The root of Docetism was the desire to make Christ more palatable to a world that sees the cross as foolishness. But the more they tried to please the world, the farther they strayed from the truth contained in Scripture.

A modern example of this can be found among classic Christian liberalism. With the dominance of science and philosophy in the nineteenth and twentieth centuries, many Christian theologians tried to make Christianity more palatable to a modern society. This is captured in the title of a book by controversial liberal bishop John Shelby Spong: *Why Christianity Must Change or Die.* Liberalism removed any literal supernaturalism (miracles, literal creation, and prophecies) in the Bible. It explained that any stories that contain supernatural elements were not historical but were mythological ways to communicate subjective experiences. New Testament scholar Rudolf Bultmann called this method of interpretation "demythologizing."

One consequence of demythologizing the Bible is to believe that the resurrection never truly happened. When it comes to the resurrection, elements of Docetism are apparent in liberalism. New Testament scholar Rudolf Bultmann thought it obvious: "The resurrection itself is not an event of past history."[13] Liberalism explains that the resurrection could merely be the disciples' nostalgia for their personal intimacy with Jesus during his earthly life. Liberalism claims that the real meaning of the resurrection is "the ethical teachings of Jesus, and ... the vague hope that the One who enunciated such principles had some personal existence beyond the grave."[14] It denies the humanness of Jesus Christ outside the tomb. This form of theological liberalism is in many ways a recapitulation of Docetism.

But this is a mistake. Paul reminds us that the cross is a stumbling block for the Jews and folly for the Gentiles, "but to those whom God has called, both Jews and Greeks, Christ the power of God and the wisdom of God" (1 Cor. 1:24).

Finally, as the author of Hebrews writes, Jesus "had to be made like them, fully human in every way, in order that he might become a merciful and faithful high priest in service to God, and that he might make atonement for the sins of the people" (Heb. 2:17). It is because he was tempted as we are that he is able to sympathize with us in our weakness. Put bluntly, the whole of the atonement rests on Docetism's being false. Twentieth-century Reformed theologian T. F. Torrance put it this way: "Any Docetic view of the humanity of Christ snaps the lifeline between God and man, and destroys the relevance of the divine acts in Jesus for men and women of flesh and blood."[15] If Docetism is true, then we no longer can place our confidence in Jesus Christ, who as truly God and truly man serves as the mediator between God and humanity.

Discussion Questions

1. How does a fully human Jesus affect our relationship to God? In particular, how does he affect the problem of our weakness and sinfulness and God's goodness?
2. Why would the Docetists insist on a God who is not fully human? What sort of benefits could you see in that arrangement?
3. What are some examples of where the authors of the New Testament go to great lengths to stress the humanity of Jesus Christ?

Further Reading

Gavrilyuk, Paul L. *The Suffering of the Impassible God: The Dialects of Patristic Thought.* Oxford Early Christian Studies. New York: Oxford Univ. Press, 2004.

Radler, Charlotte. "The Dirty Physician: Necessary Dishonor and Fleshly Solidarity in Tertullian's Writings." *Vigiliae Christianae* 63 (2009): 345–68.

Tertullianus, Quintus. *The Writings of Tertullian Vol. II,* edited by Alexander Roberts and James Donaldson. In *Ante-Nicene Christian Library,* vol. XVIII. Edinburgh: T&T Clark, 1870.

———. *The Writings of Tertullian Vol. III,* edited by Alexander Roberts and James Donaldson. In *Ante-Nicene Christian Library,* vol. XVIII. Edinburgh: T&T Clark, 1870.

CHAPTER 5

MANI

God Must Be Freed

Historical Background

In the third century, Christian ideas were swirling around the Middle East and mixing freely with other religions. The man who carried out this mixing most successfully was a religious leader named Mani, who lived in Babylonia (modern day Iraq) from 216–76 and spoke Syriac (a form of Aramaic). In the third century, Mani combined Christian, Buddhist, and Zoroastrian (Persian) doctrines to create what he considered to be the perfect religious system. Like the Gnostics, Mani believed that the spiritual realm is good and that matter is inherently evil, and he thought that he had been sent from heaven to cobble together a new faith from bits of all the major religions of his world. Although Mani's new religion was fiercely persecuted by the Persians, Romans, and Chinese, it spread rapidly from Iran both east and west — to the Chinese coast and all the way to North Africa — where it posed a serious threat to orthodox Christianity.

The Life of Mani

Mani was born somewhere in Babylonia in AD 216. Religious zeal ran in his blood — his father, Patik, had apparently made considerable personal sacrifices to convert to a Jewish-Christian sect known as the Elchaisites (founded by a Jewish Christian named El Chasai).[1] The Elchaisites retained a strict interpretation of the Jewish law in addition to a belief in Christ as a divine teacher, and they emphasized a kosher diet, a deep reverence for the environment, and baptism. Many of Mani's ideas about Christianity seem to stem from his childhood religion.

Around the age of twenty-five, Mani had a vision of an angel, who revealed to him that God had chosen him as the "Paraclete" whom Jesus promised. The angel was Mani's future glorified self, who had been appointed to protect him during his earthly mission. He explained to Mani that the true primordial religion had been corrupted by the Elchaisites and that freedom came only from separation — pure spirit had to be divorced from evil matter: "Immediately there flew down and appeared before me that most beautiful and greatest mirror-image of my self ... He delivered, separated, and pulled me away from the midst of that Law in which I was reared ... (The Twin showed Mani) who my Father on high is; or in what way, severed from him, I was sent out according to his purpose, and what sort of commission and counsel he was given to me before I clothed myself in this instrument and before I was led astray in this detestable flesh ... [He showed me] the secrets and visions and the perfections of my Father; and concerning me, who I am, and who my inseparable Twin is."[2]

Instead of expanding on the Elchaisite doctrine, Mani rebelled against it, cutting out most of the Jewish elements and elevating Christ. He rejected all of the Old Testament in addition to much of the New, and he referred to himself as "Mani, Apostle of Jesus Christ by the appointment of God the Father." To the shock of the Elchaisite community, Mani discarded kosher food rules and declared all plant foods clean. The Elchaisites, after attempting to change Mani's mind, finally cast him out.[3]

According to the Manichaean biography of Mani, he then traveled across Iran to India, where he made some converts and secured political support. It was perhaps during this journey that Mani encountered Zoroastrianism, the religion of fire that was soon to become the official religion of the Persian Empire, and Buddhism, which had made significant inroads into eastern Iran at that time. Zoroastrianism became the basis for much of Mani's view of the universe as a war between good and evil, while Buddhism influenced his ideas about the presence of God in the natural world. After spending some time in India, Mani journeyed back to Iran and won the affection of the Persian emperor, Shapur, who protected him and allowed him to spread his ideas. Followers of Mani's religion, which he claimed to be the unadulterated form of Christianity and a universal religion for both the East and West, were called Manichaeans.

Unfortunately for Mani, his success was short-lived. King Shapur soon died, and his successor, Bahram, threw Mani into prison, where he died under torture in 276.[4]

The Spread of Manichaeanism

Mani believed that by combining Buddhism and Zoroastrianism with Christianity, he could create a global religion: "The primeval religions were in one country and one language. But my religion is of that kind that it will be manifest in every country and in all languages, and it will be taught in far away countries."[5] He lived to see this vision come true; during his lifetime, Manichaean missionaries reached both Israel and Central Asia and did not stop until they had made converts from the Atlantic to the Pacific coast.

Despite the success of its missionaries, Manichaeanism never established a political system. It clashed with governments almost as a matter of course — Manichaeans were pacifist, lived introspectively, and practiced a number of alien rituals. Since they came from Iran, the Romans suspected them of being Persian spies; meanwhile, since Mani had incorporated so much of Buddhism into his system, Buddhist Chinese suspected them of being Buddhist heretics.[6] As a result, the Manichaeans were persecuted with extreme vigor in most of the lands in which they settled. Mani's ideas persisted, however. Small pockets survived up until the fourteenth century, and although Manichaeanism never made great headway in Europe, it may have influenced two great heresies of the Middle Ages, Catharism and Bogomilism, which were both dualist and antimaterial, and which both preached salvation for ordinary people by virtue of the efforts of a small cadre of the elite.[7]

Heretical Teaching

Cosmology

For Mani, the key to salvation was separation: the divine spirit was confined in the material world and needed to be released. But how did the divine spirit get there in the first place?

To answer this question, Mani developed an elaborate cosmology based on Zoroastrian dualism, the idea that good and evil are locked in an eternal battle, with neither side having the upper hand. Manichaean cosmology bears little resemblance to Christianity, but the structure of the story will be familiar to most readers. Just as the Christian story begins with the story of the fall, in which humankind rebels against God, Mani's story also begins with a fall of sorts, where darkness and light began to mingle.

In ages past, according to Mani, the kingdom of darkness launched a supernatural attack on the kingdom of light, which the kingdom of light was unable to repel entirely. God was forced to send part of himself as a soldier, known as the Primal Man, along with five gods, to battle the evil gods known as Archons. In the struggle, the Primal Man was defeated and taken captive. The Archons then created the material world to hold the Primal Man as a hostage — every plant, animal, and human contained glimmers of him. In an ingenious move, the Archons also came up with the idea of sex, which would imprison more and more pieces of God in matter as humans reproduced. Humankind is made up partly of the Primal Man, who is dazed and only faintly remembers his heritage, and partly out of the material prison.[8]

The next stage of the story involves redemption, where God begins the process of extracting Primal Man from the material world. Through messengers such as Buddha, Zoroaster, and especially Jesus (note that there are no other Jewish messengers), God tried to alert Primal Man to his condition. Most of the story of redemption involves only teaching — it is a matter of awakening a sleeping God rather than restoring a fallen nature. The story of Jesus, for instance, is framed as follows:

> [He] found the Primal Man swallowed up by darkness, him and his Five Sons ... [He] took on the aspect [form] of a sharp sword, and he allowed his shape to become visible to Primal Man, and said to him:
>
>> "Greeting, O Good Man in the midst of Evil,
>> O Creature of Light in the midst of Darkness!
>> God dwells in the midst of the beasts of wrath
>> Who do not know his honour."
>
> And the Primal Man ... said to him:
>
>> "Come with salvation, since thou bringest
>> The burden of salvation and peace...
>> How goes it with our Fathers,
>> The Sons of Light, in their City?"
>
> And the Call [i.e. Christ, the voice of God] said to him:
>
>> "It is well."[9]

Here Christ's role is primarily reminding Primal Man of his latent divinity. Christ also takes the lead in the conflict with darkness (directly after this dialogue, Christ slays the Archons), but his main duty is to make Primal Man aware that the material world is not his home.

The final stage of the cosmology involved the duties of the believers before the destruction of the world. While Christ was preaching his message, the kingdom of light organized a final counterattack. The material world would be destroyed and so, unfortunately, would the pieces of God held hostage in it. Time was running short.

The Role of the Believer in Salvation

Church historian J. N. D. Kelly describes the Manichaean view that humans are both saved by God and the savior of God: "As he exists, man is tragically involved in the material order; he is fallen and lost. Actually, however, he is a particle of Light, belonging to, though exiled from, the transcendent world. He is of the same essence as God, and human souls are fragments of the divine substance ... in the process of salvation, God is at once redeemer and redeemed."[10]

After Christ revealed to Mani that God had been trapped in an alien world, Mani organized an elite class known as the Righteous, or the Elect, to carry out the work of redeeming God. The Elect went through a lengthy purification process and lived an ascetic life, wholly dependent on the financial support of the Manichaean peasants and craftsmen, who led more or less ordinary lives. Although good works and prayer were important, the main task of the Elect was to free the pieces of God that were trapped in plants (especially cucumbers and melons, which Mani thought looked and smelled so wonderful that they must be direct links to heaven),[11] by eating them.[12] To maintain this power to free God by eating, they could not buy themselves clothes or food, and they could not have any sexual relations (having children would trap more of God in more forms of matter).[13] The freed particles of God would then drift up to heaven in a spectacular display known as "the Column of Glory."

To protect and support the Elect, Mani organized a second, much larger class known as Hearers, or Auditors. The Auditors could own property and marry, although they practiced self-restraint and birth control. Most important, they provided food for the elect and allowed them to maintain their ascetic existence. Although the Auditors were not freeing pieces of God themselves, they were guaranteed security from the coming destruction because of their care for the Elect.[14] However, this guarantee came with a twist — if the Elect slipped in their moral purity, the salvation of the Auditors would also disappear. The two classes were thus mutually dependent.

Using Mani's vision as a guide, the Elect were promised immediate access to the afterlife, where they would be freed from their material prisons and made into angels. The Auditors were offered the chance to be reincarnated as Elect or, if they were especially good, as melons (a sort of express route to heaven).[15] As far as others were concerned, the God particles would continue cycling in different forms until the final battle of good and evil took place.[16] Because all material things, including the physical body, were viewed as evil and restrictive, the Manichaeans rejected the New Testament concept of the resurrection of the dead.

Appeal

Mani's preaching is unusual, to say the least, and it might seem surprising that it won considerable support in the ancient world. To understand its appeal, think for a moment about a world without modern medicine — even basics like aspirin and penicillin. Think of how painful a toothache or an infection would be, and how there would be no prospect of relief. In such a world, it would be easy to make the blanket statement that material things are evil. And one had the option to become a Manichaean without a terrible amount of commitment by joining as an Auditor.

Those are practical reasons, but there is a theological reason as well. On the surface, Mani solved the problem of suffering very neatly. In his scheme, God is purely good and simply not all-powerful. He wants to make the world a good place, but he is thwarted by a potent evil force. The goodness of the world is trapped in evil and needs to be extracted. There is no theological difficulty over the problem of evil and the goodness of God, and little need to confront ourselves as sinners. In Christianity, humans are fallen from goodness in both body and soul, but in Manichaeanism the material part is evil in itself. This view of God and humankind is a crucial difference between Manichaeanism and orthodox Christianity.

Orthodox Response

Orthodox Christians were deeply concerned by Manichaeanism, not only because it was a highly successful rival but because it claimed to be a newer, more reliable interpretation of Christianity. Manichaeans used Christian terms and claimed Christianity's central figure, even while rejecting most of its core doctrines.

Christian theologians attacked Manichaeanism on four main grounds: first, that by stripping God of his omnipotence, Mani had also stripped him of his goodness; second, that the Manichaeans rejected God's work in history by rejecting the Old Testament; third, that Manichaeans could not accept the incarnation and thus made the work of Christ meaningless; and finally, that by placing their hopes in their efforts to free God particles, Manichaeans were looking to the wrong source for salvation.

Goodness of God

Ephrem, a Syriac Christian writer who lived on the border of the Persian Empire, had extensive contact with the Manichaeans and composed one of the better-informed refutations of their teachings. He argued that the Manichaean doctrine that the forces of evil are equally as powerful as the forces of good boils the question of good and evil down to the preference of the individual. Neither side can claim to have created the world or to have a preexisting right to rule. Instead, one side seeks the aid of humankind in gaining dominance over the other. Although Mani thought he had solved the problem of suffering and the goodness of God by removing God's absolute sovereignty, he had really made God into a politician who needed to negotiate and manipulate to get his way.[17]

Canon of Scripture

St. Augustine, a North African bishop, adhered to Manichaeanism for ten years while he was at Carthage, and then at Rome, before he converted dramatically to Christianity. After his conversion, Augustine wrote against Manichaeanism in his *Confessions* and *Against Faustus the Manichaean*. (Faustus was a chief theologian of Manichaeanism.) Although other Christian apologists, such as Hegemonius, Cyril, and Alexander of Lycopolis, made a strong case against Manichaeanism, Augustine's experience within it provided him with some of the best arguments against it.

As a young man, Augustine had been horrified by the moral failures of the Old Testament — its angry God and its ruthless wars — and its apparent crudeness.[18] This paired very well with the position of the Manichaeans, who added diplomatically that they did not feel comfortable taking for themselves a text that was written explicitly for the Jewish people.[19] However, as an older man, Augustine began to appreciate the Old Testament more. It was a nonnegotiable part of the Christian tradition, he explained, because it was written by God and foretold the coming of Christ. But more than that, it showed in physical terms the spiritual riches that would be granted in the New Testament. Only once the world had first seen how God acted in concrete things — victory in war, financial prosperity, national peace — could it then realize both God's power over every aspect of life and what God's goodness might look like spiritually even when those things were taken away: "How can you understand spiritual things of the inner man, who is renewed in the knowledge of God ... if you do not possess temporal things? You boast of despising as worthless the land of Canaan, which was an actual thing, and actually given to the Jews; and yet you tell of a land of light cut asunder on one side, as by a narrow wedge, by the land of the race of darkness."[20] By rejecting the Old Testament, the Manichaeans were missing a crucial aspect of who God is and how Christ had come to fulfill that revelation.

Work of Christ

The Manichaeans denied that Christ was really born or really suffered. They believed Christ merely made himself visible to remind the Primal Man of what he was. His sufferings were symbolic, not real, because for the Son of God to take our nature would be to contaminate himself with evil. The incarnation, as a contradiction of dualistic belief, was considered outlandish and implausible. Because of this conviction, the Manichaeans doubted the authenticity of the gospel accounts on the matter of Christ's birth, citing the conflicting genealogies of Matthew and Luke as proof that the humanity of Christ was a later invention. The only reliable information was thought to be Christ's ascetic teachings to "sell all" and live a life of devotion and self-sacrifice.

Augustine replied by pointing to the significance of Christ's death and resurrection to overcome evil. In the Manichaean account, Christ remained aloof from the material world and called to the parts of God that were trapped within. But in the New Testament, Christ entered into the material world and "became a curse" by bearing the punishment of death that God had laid on humanity.[21] Augustine maintained that the fact that Christ was a human, flesh and all, was vital to understanding how he saved humanity, and that he had taken great pains to demonstrate his material nature by inviting the apostle Thomas to touch him after the resurrection. To say otherwise was to place oneself as a higher authority than Christ.[22]

Root of Salvation

The Manichaeans argued that they were truer to Christ's teaching because they lived a purely ascetic life, while the Christians were less radical: "Faustus said: Do I believe the gospel? You ask me if I believe it, though my obedience to its commands shows that I do. I should rather ask you if you believe it, since you give no proof of your belief. I have left my father, mother, wife, and children, and all else that the gospel requires; and do you ask if I believe the gospel? Perhaps you do not know what is called the gospel. The gospel is nothing else than the preaching and the precept of Christ. I have parted with all gold and silver, and have left off carrying money in my purse; content with daily food; without anxiety for tomorrow; and without solicitude about how I shall be fed, or wherewithal I shall be clothed: and do you ask if I believe the gospel?"[23]

In terms of works, the Manichaeans were nothing if not devout. They gave their entire lives to their beliefs, and not only in consuming cucumbers to free God-particles. An ancient guide to Manichaean spirituality reveals that they were people who really tried to be temperate, to guard the environment, and to cultivate humility.[24] They were likely pleasant people. But they directed their energies to the wrong source. In response to Faustus, Augustine writes, "For the precepts, supposing you really [were] to fulfill them, would not profit you without true faith. Do you not know that the apostle says, 'If I distribute all my goods to the poor, and give my body to be burned, and have not charity, it profits me nothing?' Why do you boast of having Christian poverty, when you are destitute of Christian charity?"[25] The long list of Faustus's accomplishments was useless because he placed his trust in his radical lifestyle rather than God's love.

Of course, Manichaeanism is contrary to orthodox Christianity because it insists that there is no omnipotent God who is the creator of all things. Rather, the eternal struggle between good and evil places the force of the good on equal footing with the force of evil. In contrast, orthodox Christianity asserts that there is one God who existed prior to and separate from creation. Humanity is not part of God, and God is able to defeat evil. Colossians asserts that Christ is above every earthly power, and his victorious resurrection serves as the ultimate answer to the problem of evil. Moreover, and contrary to Manichaeanism, Christianity does not ascribe evil to creation, for the book of Genesis describes everything created by God as good before the fall of Adam.

Contemporary Relevance

Manichaeanism no longer directly influences any major religion today,[26] nor is it likely to reemerge in the West in the near future. The material comfort of Western society leaves little room for a religion that is based largely on the rejection of material things as evil, and the pragmatic, secular culture that has come to dominate the West is unlikely to embrace Mani's elaborate cosmology. However, Manichaeanism represents a few challenges, both inside and outside the church, that should be recognized.

Mani's view of salvation lay in separating darkness from light, and he drew a sharp, unambiguous distinction between the two. The doctrine has a grain of truth — we, too, believe that we are being drawn out of sin and into God's salvation; that is, we are sanctified progressively. However, while it is true that salvation is a process — that we are "being saved" — Christians are not attempting to become more and more free from their material selves. In Christ, Christians have put on a new self that renders the old fallen humanity as dead. We have newness of life in Christ, but that newness of life will fully be realized only at the final bodily resurrection, when the fullness of salvation is finally consummated.

Second, Mani's ascetic interpretation of the gospel offers a significant challenge to much contemporary consumerism and calls into question how we spend our time and money. There is no mistaking the fact that Christ calls for a simpler, less comfortable life than we would like. On the other hand, where Manichaeanism devalued the physical world as evil, the classical Christian interpretation urges us to delight in what God has created. The balance between forsaking the pleasures of the world and enjoying the goodness of creation is increasingly difficult to find in modern life.

Finally, Christians in every age must overcome one of the primary ways in which Mani stumbled — namely, in his rejection of the elements of Christianity that clashed with his own worldview and offended him. While modern Christians may laugh at the naivete of one who believes that a good person will be reincarnated as a cucumber or a melon, it is all too easy for some to overlook some of the more difficult parts of the Bible or minimize what our culture would call superstitious (such as the incarnation, the cross, the resurrection, and the ascension). We should be sure that our preferences don't dictate which parts of the Bible we consider authoritative. The central elements of the Christian faith, though standing in opposition to culturally acceptable forms of thought, are where Christians find salvation and hope.

Discussion Questions

1. Why did the Manichaeans consider the body "detestable"? Do you agree with their reasoning?
2. What are some ways in which Christians still undervalue the human body and other elements of God's good creation?
3. Manichaeans had more than good intentions — as Faustus demonstrates, they often lived intensely devout lives and professed faith in Jesus Christ. Why did ancient Christians consider them to be outside the fold of the church?
4. What attitude should a Christian have toward material things? Do you have to "sell everything and give the money to the poor" to be a Christian? If not, how might you treat material goods in a way that differs significantly from the world?

Further Reading

Augustine. *The Confessions.* Translated by Maria Boulding. New York: New City Press, 2001.
———. *Contra Faustum. http://www.newadvent.org/fathers/140604.htm.*

BeDuhn, Jason. *The Manichaean Body: In Discipline and Ritual.* Baltimore: Johns Hopkins Univ. Press, 2000.

Welburn, Andrew. *Mani, the Angel, and the Column of Glory: An Anthology of Manichaean Texts.* Edinburgh: Floris Books, 1998.

Widengren, Geo. *Mani and Manichaeanism.* Great Britain: George Weidenfeld and Nicolson, 1965.

CHAPTER 6

SABELLIUS

One Actor and Three Hats

Historical Background

During the second and third centuries, Christianity was struggling to reconcile the idea of a single God, as stated in no uncertain terms in the Old Testament — "I am the LORD, and there is no other; apart from me there is no God" (Isa. 45:5) — with the three divine names that appear at the end of the gospel of Matthew — "Therefore go and make disciples of all nations, baptizing them in the name of the Father and of the Son and of the Holy Spirit" (Matt. 28:19). What was to be done about the apparent discrepancy? If there was no God besides the God of Israel, who were the Son and the Holy Spirit? Were they new gods who had just been revealed? Was one or both somewhere in between, a demigod? Some theologians, like Marcion (see chapter 3), took the confusion as proof positive that the whole Old Testament had to be rejected, while others concluded that all three names were just three different ways that God wanted people to think of him. The most famous advocate of the latter position was a third century theologian and priest named Sabellius. Little is known about Sabellius, who was excommunicated sometime around AD 220, but the teaching attached to his name, known as Sabellianism or Sabellian Modalism, became a well-known heresy.

Heretical Teaching

Sabellianism is the most intellectually well-developed form of Modalism, a heresy that claims that the Father, Son, and Holy Spirit are simply different modes, or forms, of God rather than distinct persons. Modalism is itself a variety of an older heresy called Monarchianism, which stresses the "one rule" of God. The universe is so orderly, the Monarchians believed, that it must be the product of one supreme ruler, which means a single being. Trinitarianism seemed to complicate the idea of that single being. Monarchianism emerged as a response to the polytheism around the early Christians, affirming that there is no being equal to God and that he is the ruler over everything.[1]

While early versions of Modalism stood out as simplistic and easily dismissable, Sabellius gave the teaching a facelift, making it much more advanced and defensible. In Sabellianism, Father, Son, and Holy Spirit are just three different hats or masks that God wears, as the situation demands. Therefore, while it was proper to speak of God the Father and God the Son, it would be incorrect to refer to them as interacting with one another or having separate experiences. According to Hippolytus, an early opponent of Sabellius, Sabellianism divided up the three roles into the actions of the one God at different times in history. In other words, Father, Son, and Spirit are merely adjectives describing how the one divine being acts and is perceived by believers. Sabellius used the analogy of the sun to explain his position on the life of the Godhead. In the same way that the sun, a concrete object, gives off both light and heat, so also the single divine being radiates in history in different fashions. In the Old Testament we see the divine being acting as Father, then again in redemption in a different form as the Son in the Gospels, and finally in the lives of believers as the Holy Spirit in the present age.

Sabellius's idea raises some important questions. First, if God takes one role at a time, who was crucified? Did God actually die? And second, to whom was Jesus speaking when he referred to God the Father? The answers to these two questions made Sabellius famous. As to who died on the cross, he adopted a position that his enemies dubbed "Patripassianism" or "the suffering of the Father."[2] Sabellius was consistent with his theory of the different roles: when Scripture said that Jesus was crucified, it was referring to the same person who had made a covenant with Israel in the Old Testament as well as the one who lived with believers in the New. To buttress this point, Sabellius quoted several passages from the Old Testament, such as Isaiah 63:8–9 LXX): "He became to them deliverance out of all their affliction: not an ambassador, nor a messenger, but himself saved them, because he loved them and spared them: He himself redeemed them."[3] It seemed pretty obvious to Sabellius that the prophecy should be taken literally — the God of Israel came down and died to deliver his people, albeit in a new role.[4] He was adamant that it was all of God rather than part of God that suffered, since the point he had taken issue with in the first place was the division of God.

As for whom Jesus was addressing, Sabellius was again consistent in his theory. He proposed that Jesus was demonstrating how to pray for our benefit rather than holding an actual conversation with God. Sabellius used Jesus' words to Philip at the Last Supper as a prooftext: "Don't you know me, Philip, even after I have been among you such a long time? Anyone who has seen me has seen the Father. How can you say, 'Show us the Father'?" (John 14:9). This passage should have priority over the prayer, Sabellius believed, because Jesus was clearly identifying what the nature of God is. The idea that Jesus was praying as a demonstration was also related to Sabellius's interpretation of "the Word" in John 1; while acknowledging that John 1 seems to hint at the divinity of the Word (traditionally seen as Christ by the orthodox), Sabellius maintained that the Word was to be understood in the simplest sense, as a sound that God had made, rather than turning the Word into a person.[5]

Sabellius's writings do not survive — the previously quoted passages are taken from quotations preserved by his opponents — and it is difficult to pin down his theology in its best form. It is also unclear what led him to develop his theory. However, from what we can glean from the reactions of his opponents, he had several legitimate concerns. Naturally, he wanted to defend the oneness of God. At this time, several groups had split from Christianity that proclaimed two or more gods — Marcion, for instance, or the Gnostics (see chapter 2). Many of these groups had thrown out Christianity's Jewish heritage. By prioritizing oneness, Modalists were voting for continuity with Judaism and in particular with Jewish monotheism. The fact that God the Father and God the Son (as the Trinitarians put it) each had their own testament only invited division. Marcion had published a list of differences between what he saw as the personalities of the God of the Old Testament and the God of the New, and declared his allegiance to the God of the New. But what if both books were actually devoted to the same God in different roles? The discrepancies would be resolved. Furthermore, Sabellians defended the full divinity of Christ against what they saw as a worrying tendency to demote him to a demigod.[6] Earlier theologians such as Hippolytus had made claims that Christ and God the Father were two persons; Sabellians must have considered the division too sharp, and they charged Hippolytus and others like him with ditheism (worshiping two gods).[7]

Some of Sabellius's concerns were pastoral. Sabellius thought that the idea of assigning persons to the three names was overly complicated in a way that God himself would not be. Perhaps the Trinity was a distinction that specialized theologians could make, but for the uneducated laypeople who made up the bulk of the church, a God who is both three and one would be impossible to worship without drifting into polytheism.[8] So in addition to trying to maintain Jewish monotheism, Sabellius thought that his theory of "simple Unity" was a way to take Christianity out of the hands of academics and put it back where it belonged.

Sabellianism persisted in the outer regions of the Roman Empire for some time (especially in Libya, Sabellius's homeland), and was condemned at most church councils. Although its theology was influential, largely because it was so easy to grasp, Sabellianism lacked clout as a movement and never made much headway into the church proper. The closest it came to doing so was when Sabellius managed to gain favor with Pope Callistus, a rival of Sabellius's arch-enemy Hippolytus, but Callistus soon excommunicated Sabellius and ended his career in the public eye.[9]

However, Sabellianism was indirectly credited with creating a much bigger theological crisis in the following centuries. Arianism, which drew sharp distinctions between Father, Son, and Holy Spirit, was in many ways the opposite of the Sabellian heresy. It was rumored that Arius, who had formerly been a Christian monk, developed overly strong views on the distinctions among the Godhead after hearing what he considered to be a Sabellian sermon in Egypt.[10] Indeed, Arianism represented most of the criticisms that Sabellius leveled against the Trinitarians, including the division of God into multiple beings.

Orthodox Response

In theology, it is much easier to tell when an idea is wrong than it is to articulate precisely the right answer. The church had been adamant that Modalism did not adequately account for the way God had revealed himself in Scripture, but as of yet few theologians had advanced a solution that was adequate. The challenge of Sabellianism and its brief influence in high places motivated the first substantial Trinitarian theologies and generated the terms that we use today.

The orthodox party was represented by three major figures: Hippolytus, a failed candidate for pope, Tertullian, a North African lawyer and convert to Christianity, and Origen, a brilliant but eccentric philosopher from Egypt. Together, these figures hammered out the basics of Trinitarian theology that later figures, such as Athanasius, improved upon.

The Sabellians maintained that any Scripture passage that suggests that God is more than one must be interpreted metaphorically. But Tertullian argued that a metaphorical interpretation twisted the terms "Father" and "Son," which were given to humans to convey something real about God. "In order to be a husband, I must have a wife," Tertullian said. "I can never myself be my own wife. In like manner, in order to be a father, I have a son, for I never can be a son to myself; and in order to be a son, I have a father, it being impossible for me ever to be my own father."[11] Furthermore, he showed that Christ showed his deity to the apostles not only by assuming the attributes of the God of Israel (such as when he says, "I am," in John 8:58) but also by calling on God the Father as a separate witness. Quoting John 8:18, Tertullian writes, "'I am one who am bearing witness of myself; and the Father (is another) who has sent me, and bears witness of me.' Now, if he were one — being at once both the Son and the Father — he certainly would not have quoted the sanction of the law, which requires not the testimony of one, but of two."[12] The fact that Christ did not know when the end of the world would take place, the fact that he was forsaken by God on the cross, and the fact that he constantly pointed his listeners to the Father as well as himself all rendered Sabellius's theory difficult to maintain.

However, it remained for the orthodox party to explain precisely what Christ is in relation to the Father, and this was the real achievement of the controversy. They agreed that there are not two gods, as Marcion and some of the Gnostics said. Tertullian therefore developed terms that emphasized the unity of God as well as his distinctions. He proposed that we speak of the Godhead as "one substance (*substantia*) consisting in three persons (*persona*)," which was rendered in Greek as *ousia* (essence or being) and *hypostases* (concrete things).[13] That way, God can be understood properly as one being, a single agent, but it can also be acknowledged that God is also three persons who interact with one another and work together. It is from Tertullian that we get the important Christian word "Trinity," although the idea of the Trinity had been around long before and is taught in the Bible.

Tertullian and Origen also set forth explanations of how a Trinity might be possible without creating demigods. They proposed that Christ eternally proceeds from the Father, rather than being born at a single moment in time. (The Sabellians had accused the orthodox of embracing the Valentinian heresy, which said that God created a number of lesser gods, or Aeons.) Although "begotten" suggests a one-time, completed action in the past, Tertullian pointed out that God is said to beget Wisdom in Proverbs 8:22 — a personified, speaking Wisdom — but was there a time when God was without or will be without Wisdom?[14] Surely not. God does not have to create his own insight — it simply flows out of him. Similarly, it is possible to "beget" the Son of God without meaning that God created a separate god.[15] Christ came from, was dependent on, and was inextricably linked to the Father: "I confess that I call God and His Word — the Father and His Son — two. For the root and the tree are distinctly two things, but correlatively joined; the fountain and the river are also two forms, but indivisible; so likewise the sun and the ray are two forms, but coherent ones. Everything which proceeds from something else must needs be second to that from which it proceeds, without being on that account separated. Where, however, there is a second, there must be two; and where there is a third, there must be three. Now the Spirit indeed is third from God and the Son; just as the fruit of the tree is third from the root."[16]

However, even if this is so, why not speak of a divine Triad? Should we refer to God as the three persons of the Trinity, as "them" instead of "him"? Tertullian argued that when Jesus said, "I and my Father are one," he was emphasizing the idea of substance, or divine essence, that allows us to refer to God as a single being. The phrase meant more than the mere unity of purpose that two separate beings would have, even if it also meant less than the complete identification of the Father with the Son that Sabellius had suggested. Instead, Christ was saying that he and the Father are one being, and that the idea that God is a single being came first: to talk to Christ, for example, is to talk to all the members of the Trinity.[17] The later Athanasian Creed puts it this way:

1. [W]e worship one God in Trinity, and Trinity in Unity;
2. Neither confounding the persons nor dividing the substance.
3. For there is one person of the Father, another of the Son, and another of the Holy Spirit.
4. But the Godhead of the Father, of the Son, and of the Holy Spirit is all one, the glory equal, the majesty coeternal.
5. Such as the Father is, such is the Son, and such is the Holy Spirit.

Since God is one, it is possible to distinguish the members of the Trinity, but that distinction does not affect worshiping God as a whole. Jesus' glory is also the Father's glory, and so forth. Many of the ideas listed above appeared in Tertullian's work during this controversy.

Contemporary Relevance

Sabellianism is one of the heresies in the church that sticks around. Anyone who has sat in a Sunday school class and heard that God is like water because he can take three forms (liquid, steam, and ice) has been exposed to a contemporary variation of Modalism. God is not one person who can change into three different forms but a being who is complex within himself.

Although it generally has a low profile compared to Arianism, Modalism has also gained some momentum. It is seen today in the oneness Pentecostalism movement, which denies the Trinity.

However, Modalism gains ground less because it is strongly advocated than because of apathy. Sabellianism is attractive in its simplicity, and Sabellius's pastoral challenge — that the Trinity is the province of specialized theologians — strikes a chord in modern culture. Compared with the idea that God is merely one, the orthodox answer might seem overly complex and philosophical, or an unnecessary later addition to the authentic Christian faith. After all, the Bible does not spell out the Trinity — though it is clearly taught from passages from all over Scripture.[18]

Perhaps one of the best reasons for complex Trinitarianism comes from C. S. Lewis, who once wrote, "Good philosophy must exist, if for no other reason, because bad philosophy needs to be answered."[19] In some respects, this describes the Sabellian controversy; orthodox philosophy needed to be developed to answer the Sabellian philosophy. But Trinitarian theology is much more than a merely human philosophy. It takes seriously the idea that God has revealed himself in Scripture and wants to be known, and that he has revealed himself in a certain way. The question at the beginning of the chapter — *only* one God, or three? — is unavoidable when reading the Bible, and the consequence of leaving the question unanswered is to let it be badly answered.

Sabellianism was one such bad answer. In the Sabellian scheme, God is no longer love, because he no longer has anyone whom he has loved eternally. The intimate relationship between God the Father and Jesus in John 17 becomes a weird sort of schizophrenia. Finally, since God takes on several different roles as he pleases (such as Son and Father), it is questionable whether we have ever encountered God as he really is rather than what he does. The orthodox party — laboriously, with many starts and stops in the first few centuries — worked out the answer that is best in accord with Scripture.

What's more, Modalism undercuts the atoning work of Jesus Christ. If there is only one God who merely appears in different forms in history, one must question whether Jesus Christ was truly man, or if he only appeared to be, as in the heresy of Docetism. If Jesus Christ is not fully God and fully man, then he cannot be the one mediator between God and man.

On a final, practical note, some other religions, particularly the Jehovah's Witnesses and Mormons, see Christianity as Sabellian.

Since many of the errors that these groups ascribe to mainstream Christianity are actually Sabellian in nature, it is useful to know the middle road that orthodox doctrine strikes between unity and distinction. Being able to articulate concisely what the Trinity is, how it makes the best sense of Scripture, and how it affects our salvation and the worship of God can be valuable in witnessing to others as well as developing our own relationship with God.

Discussion Questions

1. What do you make of Sabellius's pastoral challenge? Does the doctrine of the Trinity overcomplicate matters? How would you introduce solid Trinitarian theology to others?
2. Why do you think Sabellianism, with its idea that God is merely one, was less of a problem for the church than other heresies?
3. Sabellius placed a great deal of weight on the Old Testament prophecies that God would come to Israel. How would an orthodox interpretation of those prophecies differ from Sabellius? What difference would that make in our understanding of God?

Further Reading

Bickersteth, Edward Henry. *The Trinity: The Classical Study of Biblical Trinitarianism.* Grand Rapids, MI: Kregel, 2000.

Hippolytus. *A Refutation of All Heresies,* Book IX. *http://www.newadvent.org/fathers/050109.htm.*

Letham, Robert. *The Holy Trinity: In Scripture, History, Theology, and Worship.* Phillipsburg, NJ: P&R, 2004.

Tertullian. *Against Praxeas. http://www.newadvent.org/fathers/0317.htm.*

CHAPTER 7

ARIUS
Jesus Is a Lesser God

Historical Background

Sudden chaos overtook Alexandria in 318. A riot broke out and people streamed into the street chanting, "There was a time when Christ was not!" Meanwhile, another large group of Christians stood their ground with the bishop against this movement, insisting that Christ is the eternal God along with the Father. Eventually this conflict spilled over to the rest of the empire and threatened to break apart the unity of the church. What began this crisis? It really came down to one man — Arius (ca. 256–336).

Arius was a presbyter in Alexandria, the home of the brilliant theologian Origen (184–230). He came under the influence of Lucian of Antioch, a headmaster at a Christian school, and went to school with Eusebius of Nicomedia, who eventually became an important and influential bishop. Arius eventually went on to become a presbyter in Alexandria. Like most in Antioch, all three erred on the side of emphasizing the humanity of Christ rather than his divinity. They firmly rejected Sabellius's Modalism (see chapter 6), because that would imply that God the Father died and was crucified on the cross. And lest they put their respective church positions in jeopardy, they knew they could not publicly embrace Paul of Samosata's

Adoptionism (the idea that a human person named Jesus was adopted into divinity). A new solution needed to be developed. Based partly on Origen's teachings on the Trinity, Arius developed a theory of the nature of God that firmly separated Jesus from the Father.

Since part of Arius's responsibility as presbyter was to direct a school of biblical interpretation for priests and laypersons who wished to teach, his theories quickly gained traction with the next generation of Christian leaders. Over time he began to openly criticize Alexander, bishop of Alexandria. Alexander has been described in history as a gentle and tolerant soul who did not relish conflicts. Nevertheless, the bishop took the field against Arius and insisted that the Son is just as much God as the Father. Arius then accused Alexander of being sympathetic to Sabellius's Modalism.

A time came when the Arian movement became so popular that Alexander could no longer fight Arius's criticism with mere sermons and correspondences. He called a synod of bishops to discuss whether Arius's views were orthodox. Before they made a decision, Arius rallied his followers to pour out into the streets to add pressure to the leaders. Arius's sympathizers wrote songs to fire up the working class. The mob got caught up in the passion of the slogans, songs, and Arius's personality, but they did not necessarily grasp the theological issues. In response, Alexander's supporters likewise marched in the streets against Arius. When the two groups met, a riot broke out.

But the synod went on. More than a hundred bishops from various parts of the eastern Roman Empire listened to Alexander critique Arius's teachings. He accused Arius of resurrecting Paul of Samosata's Adoptionism in a more sophisticated way. It did not matter whether the Logos was created before or after time began, Alexander argued. The difference was slight. The fact of the matter was that Arius denied the deity of Christ, which is why Paul of Samosata's teaching was rejected. Alexander insisted that salvation depends on God's uniting himself with humanity in the person of Jesus Christ so that we can be saved. After hearing this, the synod decided that Arius's view was heretical and forced him to leave the city.

Heretical Teaching

Arius was not trying to start a crisis; he thought that the relationship between God and Jesus was simple and needed to be freed from overcomplication. After all, "Trinity" was not a common term at the time, and it had not yet been precisely defined. The word "Trinity" is not found in Scripture (it was first used by Tertullian), and it is best described as shorthand for all the teachings of Scripture on the nature of God. Since the age of the apostles, Jesus had always been considered divine in at least some sense, but his precise relationship to the Godhead had not yet been articulated. Yet the church still had an unspoken sense of what the Trinity *isn't*. This was why Sabellius was rejected for teaching that God is sometimes the Father, at other times the Son, and then at another time the Spirit, but never all at once (Modalism). Paul of Samosata, likewise, was rejected, because he taught that Jesus started out as a mere man who was "adopted" by God to become the Son of God (Adoptionism). Those early explanations were deemed incompatible with Scripture and therefore heresies.

Arius's own conceptions of the Trinity can be traced back to Origen (184–253), a brilliant and imaginative Egyptian theologian.[1] Two streams of thought flowed in Origen's teachings concerning the Son, and followers gravitated to one of the two streams. In one stream, Origen strongly affirmed that the Son is equal to the Father. In the other stream, Origen wrote that the Son is eternally subordinate to the Father. The implication of the second stream communicated to some that the Son is somehow a lesser being than the Father, though Origen did not elaborate.[2] The lack of a fuller explanation of the second stream of Origen's thought left the door wide open for further suggestions.

To understand Arius's theory, we must mention two common presumptions about God that were derived from the logic of Greek philosophy. First, God does not change (immutability). Change implies imperfection. For good or bad, if God changes, then he cannot be deemed absolutely perfect because he has either improved or regressed. God is already at the peak of perfection, so there is no room to grow, and he is fixed at that peak of perfection, so he cannot regress. Second, the other presumption is that God cannot suffer; he is "passionless" (impassibility). Most early theologians believed in these two attributes of God.

Arius and his followers exploited these two attributes to advance their argument that the Son is not coeternal with the Father but is the supreme creation. He acknowledged that everyone believed that Jesus Christ is the incarnation of the *Logos* (the Word). No problem there. The problem lay with the following: "If the Logos is divine in the same sense that God the Father is divine, then God's nature would be changed by the human life of Jesus in time and God would have suffered in him."[3] The implication that God changes and suffers seemed blasphemous! So it must be then, Arius concluded, that only God the Father is without beginning. The Son came into existence through the will of the Father. To avoid charges of Adoptionism, Arius taught that the *Logos* was begotten "timelessly"[4] — that is, before Genesis 1:1. "In the beginning," the *Logos* was created and was given all things from the Father to share.[5] With this solution it was not God the Father who grew up and eventually suffered on the cross but only the *Logos* experienced this on behalf of God and humanity. Thus, when the Scriptures speak of Jesus as the Son of God, this is merely a title of honor — a title given to Jesus as the one on whom the Father had lavished a special grace.

Arius believed that the Father and the Son are two separate beings and that the biblical model for their relationship is one of eternal subordination: the Father is the one who decides matters and the Son is the one who obeys. That the Son would yield to the Father's preferences was a natural conclusion, since in Arius's model the Son is simply a loyal creature serving his creator.

Arius explained the sharpness of his division in reasonable terms: "For God to implant His substance to some other being, however exalted, would imply that He is divisible and subject to change, which is inconceivable. Moreover, if any other being were to participate in the divine nature in any valid sense, there would result a duality of divine beings, whereas the Godhead is by definition unique."[6] According to Arius, if the Father and the Son were of the same essence, it is difficult to see how in the incarnation the Father would not become passible.

Arius argued that the Son was created before time. He is not coeternal with the Father. As he put it, "Before he was begotten or created or appointed or established, he did not exist; for he was not unbegotten."[7] Furthermore, the Son is not of one divine substance with the Father. He is rather of a similar substance with the Father (Greek *homoiousios*). On this view, the divine qualities of the Son are derivative (contingent, not essential), given to the Son by the Father. As Arius described Jesus, "He is not God truly, but by participation in grace ... He too is called God in name only."[8]

Orthodox Response

The Arian division caught Emperor Constantine's attention. Although Christianity was not the official religion, Constantine hoped to use Christianity as a glue to hold the already shaky empire together. As Christianity went, so went the empire. Thus, he called the Council of Nicaea in 325 to resolve the situation.[9] After dramatic rounds of debates, the majority in the council stood with Alexander and condemned Arianism. They added to the Apostle's Creed precise wording to clearly denounce Arianism with the following: "We believe ... in one Lord Jesus Christ, the Son of God, begotten from the Father [only-begotten; that is, of the essence of the Father, God of God], Light of Light, very God of very God, begotten not made, being of one substance [*homoousious*] with the Father ..."[10]

They adopted the term *homoousious*, meaning, "of the same substance," to describe the Son's relation to the Father. This horrified the Arians, but the orthodox bishops, such as Alexander and his young protege Athanasius, were overjoyed. However, even this council could not quell the rising popularity of Arianism. In fact the council served as a catalyst for it to grow even more rapidly! So much so that Constantine began to doubt the wording of the Nicene Creed and thought about rewriting it in favor of Arianism. One man stood in his way: Athanasius (ca. 296–373).

The torch passed on from Alexander to Athanasius to defend orthodoxy even when it was starting to become unpopular. Elected as the new Bishop of Alexandria in 328, Athanasius found it appalling that Arius insisted that the Son is a creature. He had no time for Arius's "smooth sophistry."[11] A creature is a creature. What other types of creatures are there? Athanasius argued two negative consequences make Arianism dangerous and unacceptable.[12]

First, Athanasius argued that only God can save humanity. No creature can cancel the power of sin and death, and thereby offer eternal life to other creatures. Only the Creator can do this. So he argued that Arianism makes salvation impossible, because — no matter how high his status — the Son is still only a creature. Since everybody in the church recognizes that Jesus Christ saves, it stands to reason that Jesus is therefore God.

Second, looking at the common liturgy taking place in the fourth century, it was clear that the church prayed to and worshiped Jesus Christ. If the Son is only a creature, then the church is making a grave mistake in its public worship. Clearly, the first of the Ten Commandments forbids the people of God from worshiping anything else but God. If Arianism were true, Christians were committing idolatry.[13] The church should not be worshiping Christ if he is merely a creature. So either Arians are right in their doctrine of the Son or the Church is right in its practice of worshiping the Son. Both cannot be right. Athanasius argued the church was right to worship the Son, because the Son is God.[14]

Athanasius called the heresy of Arius the "forerunner of the Antichrist."[15] Athanasius proposed an alternative interpretation: since God created the world through Christ, and since Christ alone is said to be from the Father, it is proper to understand Christ and the Father as both being God.[16]

According to Athanasius, the Son was eternally begotten from the Father such that he can be said to be of the same essence (*homoousios*) with the Father: "The Son is other in kind and nature than the creatures, or rather belongs to the Father's substance and is of the same nature as He."[17] Although the word "begotten" (which Athanasius borrowed from John 3:16) might suggest a one-time event, Athanasius relied on the unchanging nature of God to explain that the Father is eternally begetting and the Son is eternally begotten. If that sounds confusing, remember Tertullian's early analogy of the different parts of a tree. There is the root, which carries water into the trunk, which then distributes it to the branches — a constant process as long as the tree is alive.

Moreover, Athanasius heavily emphasized the idea of salvation through *theosis*, a concept that had been popular with Origen and other Alexandrian intellectuals of his day. The doctrine of *theosis* said that the ultimate purpose of salvation is to make humans godlike — the image of God in humankind would be made pristine. It's roughly equivalent to what Protestant churches call "glorification." According to Athanasius, it is nonsensical to say that a nondivine creature could make others divine. His thoughts are worth quoting in full:

> For humanity would not have been deified if joined to a creature, or unless the Son were true God. Nor would humanity have been drawn into the Father's presence, unless the one who had put on the body was the true Word by nature. And as we would not have been delivered from sin and the curse, unless it had been by nature human flesh which the Word put on (for we would have had nothing in common with what was foreign), so also humanity would not have been deified, unless the Word who became flesh had been by nature from the Father and true and proper to him ... Therefore let those who deny that the Son is from the Father by nature and proper to his essence deny also

that he took true human flesh of Mary Ever-Virgin. For in neither case would it have profited us human beings, if the Word had not been true Son of God by nature, or the flesh not true which he assumed.[18]

Defending his arguments proved to be a difficult task for Athanasius. In 332, Constantine restored Arius to his position as presbyter under immense political pressure. Athanasius was asked to accept this, but he refused. So he was exiled to the farthest outpost in Germany. Along his way to his exile, he met with several bishops in the West. They began to favor his view and Athanasius was seen as somewhat of a hero for standing up to Constantine. Disappointments, after all, still brewed in the West over the moving of the capitol from Rome to Constantinople.

So, ironically, Athanasius's exile helped bring back momentum for orthodoxy. Not only was Athanasius building up a network of support in the West but the church in Alexandria refused to replace Athanasius. So he was still technically a bishop. Arius never did return to his position; he died a day before he was to be reinstalled (336). Constantine died a few months later (337).

Constantine's son and successor, Constantius, allowed Athanasius to return to his position in Alexandria. But their relationship was a tumultuous one. Constantius, like his father, wanted stability for the empire. To maintain this, he thought the Semi-Arian view could be a good compromise between the Arians and the orthodox doctrines. They proposed replacing the word *homoousious* (meaning "of the same substance") with the word *homoiousious* (meaning "of similar substance"). The words were differentiated in Latin by one little letter. Surely, Constantius thought, there is no harm in compromising with some slight differences.

To Athanasius, this was no small matter. That little letter made all the difference in the world in understanding how the Father relates to the Son. Salvation depends on Christ's being God, not "like God." He still insisted only God can save humanity. He argued that "salvation is not ... possible through an hierarchical chain, from the Father through an intermediate Son to creatures. For an intermediary separates as much as he unites creatures with the Father."[19] The essentials to the gospel remained: Jesus Christ must be truly God and truly human in order to be the perfect mediator.

Athanasius had to endure five exiles. In his forty-six years as bishop, he spent only seventeen in Alexandria. But he stubbornly stuck to the truth despite being up against what seemed like the world, and he is now recognized as perhaps the foremost defender of Nicene orthodoxy and the most prolific writer of orthodox Trinitarian doctrine in the fourth century. A few years after he died, his friends, the Cappadocian fathers — Basil the Great, Gregory of Nyssa, and Gregory of Nazianzus — carried the torch to win the fight against Arianism and Semi-Arianism at the Council of Constantinople in 381.

Contemporary Relevance

When it comes to the Trinity, a helpful caution might be in order. We can and should confess what the Trinity is, but no matter how deep we may probe into God's nature, we cannot possibly begin to understand it fully. Evangelical theologian Harold O. J. Brown elaborates:

> Without a coherent doctrine of the Trinity, the New Testament witness to the activity of God in Christ and in the work of the Holy Spirit will tend to force one either into modalism or a kind of tritheism. But if one begins with a doctrine of Trinity — as a number of orthodox Protestant theologians do — there is the danger that doctrine will take precedence over the New Testament witness and turn living, personal faith into theological metaphysics. It seems apparent that the safest course is to let theological understanding and personal faith go hand in hand. Too much enthusiastic faith without a corresponding degree

of theological understanding is almost certain to lead to error, perhaps to serious heresy. Too much doctrine unaccompanied by a living and growing faith is the recipe for dead orthodoxy.[20]

Though we can apprehend the doctrine of the Trinity, we cannot fully comprehend it. Despite that fact, it is vital to maintain a Trinitarian faith. As seen earlier, the doctrine of the Trinity impacts one's understanding of salvation. Additionally, it also affects the way we worship.[21]

Athanasius saw the deity of Christ and the Trinity as essential to the practice of the church. Not only were baptismal and Eucharistic confessions bound up in Trinitarian language but so also were prayers. The Son was adored, prayed to, and believed to be present in the Eucharist, and if he was not really God, the worshipers were depriving God of the worship which is his due. But more than this, Athanasius saw that if the Son were not divine, the salvation of humans was called into question. In the same way that Gregory of Nazianzus argued that Jesus Christ must be fully human (as opposed to the claims of Apollinarianism in chapter 8) if he were to be the mediator between God and men, Athanasius argued that Jesus must be fully divine:

> "For it became Him, for Whom are all things, and through Whom are all things, in bringing many sons unto glory, to make the Captain of their salvation perfect through suffering;" by which words He means that it belonged to none other to bring man back from the corruption which had begun, than the Word of God, Who had also made them from the beginning. And that it was in order to [become] the sacrifice for bodies such as His own that the Word Himself also assumed a body, to this, also, they refer in these words: "Forasmuch then as the children are the sharers in blood and flesh, He also Himself in like manner partook of the same, that through death He might bring to naught Him that had the power of death, that is, the devil; and might deliver them who, through fear of death, were all their lifetime subject to bondage."[22]

Athanasius saw an intimate connection between the salvation of humanity and the deity of Christ. Even though some sects like the Jehovah's Witnesses still repeat elements of Arian teaching, Jesus claimed to be God, and the Christian tradition has maintained Athanasius's belief in an intimate connection between salvation and the deity of Christ.

We are saved from God by God. Only a divine Savior can bear the weight of God's wrath in atonement. Only Jesus as the God-man can satisfy the enormous debt and penalty caused by human sin against God. No mere human could bridge that gap. Only a divine Savior can pay the costly price for redeeming us from our bondage to sin and death. Only the God-man can conquer all his people's enemies. Our salvation is dependent on the infinite divine capacity of our Savior, Jesus Christ.

Discussion Questions

1. If the Father is totally separate from the Son, does that change how he treats the Son? Put another way, does Arianism invite the charges of "cosmic child abuse" that critics level against God the Father? Read John 10:14–18. How does Trinitarianism resolve those criticisms?
2. Is it appropriate to pray to Jesus or to the Holy Spirit? Does this look different from praying to the Father?
3. What does salvation look like in Arianism? How is this different from the way that orthodox Trinitarians interpret salvation?

Further Reading

Anatolios, Khaled. *Retrieving Nicaea: The Development and Meaning of Trinitarian Doctrine.* Grand Rapids, MI: Baker Academic, 2011.

Athanasius. *Four Discourses against the Arians.* http://www.newadvent.org/fathers/2816.htm.

Ayres, Lewis. *Nicaea and Its Legacy: An Approach to Fourth Century Trinitarian Theology.* Oxford: Oxford Univ. Press, 2006.

Hanson, R. P. C. *The Search for the Christian Doctrine of God: The Arian Controversy, 318–381.* Grand Rapids, MI: Baker Academic, 2006.

Leithart, Peter J. *Athanasius.* Foundations of Theological Exegesis and Christian Spirituality. Grand Rapids, MI: Baker Academic, 2011.

Newman, John Henry Cardinal. *The Arians of the Fourth Century.* London: Longmans, 1919.

Pettersen, Alvyn. *Athanasius.* Harrisburg, PA: Morehouse, 1995.

Rusch, William G., ed. and trans. *The Trinitarian Controversy.* Sources of Early Christian Thought. Minneapolis: Fortress, 1980.

Williams, Rowan. *Arius: Heresy and Tradition.* Grand Rapids, MI: Eerdmans, 2002.

CHAPTER 8

APOLLINARIUS

Christ May Be Human, but His Mind Is Divine

Historical Background

In the years following the Council of Nicaea in AD 325, the church wrestled with many important questions about the person and work of Christ. Nicaea established the deity of Christ as orthodox Christian teaching by framing certain Trinitarian statements. The Nicene Creed confessed Jesus' deity as "very God of very God" and confirmed his humanity as "the man Jesus Christ." Emperor Constantine convened the council at Nicaea to resolve church divisions over Arian teachings that Christ was not fully God but was indeed fully human. This controversy prompted theologians to state unambiguously that Jesus was the eternal, preexistent Son of God. At the same time, heresies such as Docetism (see chapter 4) and Gnosticism (see chapter 2) compelled the council to be clear that Jesus was really a man, not one in appearance only. The question that remained was, How could the nature of Christ's humanity relate to the nature of his deity in a single person? A heated debate raged on for the next hundred years or so until the Council of Chalcedon (AD 451), which provided a definition of the relationship of the human and divine in Christ.

This debate can be divided into two schools of thought: the Alexandrian school and the Antiochene school. During the first few centuries AD, the cities of Alexandria in Egypt and Antioch in Syria produced some of the most sophisticated theological minds in early Christianity. The tendency in Alexandria was to emphasize what happened to the human nature when God became man. They asserted that God was interested in making humans godlike, so they tended to emphasize the fact that Christ had created something entirely new by taking on a human nature. The Alexandrian approach is often referred to by scholars as a "Word-flesh" Christology, because it was focused on how Christ had changed what it means to be human. In contrast, the thought in Antioch preferred to view the two natures of Christ as distinct: "God became incarnate in this person and took *him* on, not *it* (a mere human nature)."[1] Scholars often call the Antiochene view a "Word-man" Christology because the Antiochenes wanted to emphasize the fact that Christ's humanity included a mind and human desires.

Of course, extreme versions of each school of thought resulted in heretical error. The theology of Nestorius took Antiochene theology so far as to separate the natures of Christ and potentially create two persons. Apollinarius (d. 390) took Alexandrian theology to the point of blurring the distinctions between the natures.

Each of these errors compromises important teachings about salvation. For instance, if there are two persons in Jesus, how can he truly be the one mediator between God and man? Moreover, if the unity of Jesus' person is overemphasized, such that the *Logos* (his divine principle) replaced his rational soul and merely drove his body around (thereby serving as the animating principle of his person), then it is questionable whether Jesus is fully human. That is, if he has no human soul, he did not become truly and entirely human. This is the error of Apollinarius.

Heretical Teaching

According to Gregory of Nazianzus, Apollinarianism can be traced to as early as AD 352. Apollinarius, named Bishop of Laodicea in 362, was a devoted opponent of Antiochene Christology. Apollinarius brought the debate between Alexandrian and Antiochene Christology to the public with his teachings. As Bishop of Laodicea, he tried to teach his church how Jesus could be truly human and truly God. He vigorously rejected subordinationism, which taught that since the Son and the Holy Spirit proceed from the Father, they are not fully divine. He attributed this heresy to the Antiochene school, therefore he would not hear of any talk about two distinct natures in Christ. He appealed to Nicaea and emphasized the full deity of the man Jesus Christ. More than an illuminated man, "he delighted to speak of Christ as 'God-incarnate,' 'flesh-bearing God,' or 'God born into a woman.'"[2] To Apollinarius, salvation was at stake here. If Christ was merely a man, then he could not save humanity. He would not be worthy of worship. His deity must be defended! However, in his attempt to emphasize Christ's deity, he overreached by overly deemphasizing Christ's humanity.

There are two assumptions we must understand about Apollinarius before getting into what he contributed to the debate.

1. Concerning human nature, Apollinarius was influenced by Plato and understood human nature to be composed of three aspects: a body, a sensitive soul, and a rational mind. Apollinarius would argue that the Bible teaches the same concept using the language of body, soul, and spirit (1 Thess. 5:23). To him, the body and the soul made up the lower part of nature as the life force; the rational intellectual mind was identified as part of the higher nature known as the mind or consciousness.

2. Concerning the divine nature, Apollinarius emphasized the teaching that God does not change (immutable), cannot suffer (impassible), and is all-knowing (omniscient). He considered it blasphemous then to suggest that God could be made into a weak and limited human being susceptible to any kind of suffering. God has no beginning and is not about to begin

something new in his nature at any point in history, so Christ must possess the divine traits from the beginning.

With these two presuppositions in mind, the question then was "into what kind of flesh can God be made?"[3] Apollinarius answered that Jesus Christ took on humanity only to the extent of assuming a human body and a sensitive soul. The *Logos*, or eternal Son, replaced the rational intellectual soul that would have existed in a normal human person, which meant that the person of Jesus Christ lacked an important piece of human nature. As Stephen Nichols summarizes Apollinarius's view, "In order to preserve Christ's deity, Apollinarius was unwilling to grant that Christ has a human will, which for him could be nothing but sinful, and therefore Christ did not have a human rational soul."[4]

One could say then that Jesus, as Apollinarius described him, was only two-thirds human. But that didn't bother Apollinarius.[5] After all, Jesus was conceived by the Holy Spirit, rather than through ordinary biology. The full humanity of Christ was not necessary to Apollinarius's doctrine of salvation because it had nothing to do with the infinite power of Christ to make man more and more like God (a special focus of the fourth century).

The simplicity of Apollinarianism quickly caused it to gain popularity among Trinitarians and heretics alike. "It could 'work' whether one believed the Son of God who dwelled in Jesus Christ as his rational soul was eternal God or created demigod," observes Roger Olson.[6] However, Apollinarius did not think he was inventing anything new. He thought he was just teaching the same doctrines prior orthodox theologians had taught, but in a better way.[7]

Unfortunately, by suggesting that the eternal Word of God (the *Logos*) replaced the human rational soul of the man Jesus, Apollinarianism compromised the full humanity of Jesus. If Jesus was said to be human, Apollinarius reasoned, it could not be in the usual sense, because his humanity depended on his divinity. Thus, Jesus was human in the sense that his human side "leaned on" his divine side — where there was a question about whether his mind or his will was human or divine, the divine part automatically overruled the human part.[8]

Kelly points out the problem: "The frankly acknowledged presupposition of this argument is that the divine Word was substituted for the normal human psychology in Christ."[9] Put differently, the humanity that was assumed in the incarnation was not a complete humanity but lacked a significant component of personhood. If Apollinarius is right, then Jesus was only partially human.

Orthodox Response

As word got around concerning Apollinarius's innovative teaching, opposition came out of the woodwork. First, Pope Damascus of Rome in 377 held a council to condemn Apollinarius outright. After this, the dominoes fell rapidly in the synods of Alexandria (378) and Antioch (379) to confirm Rome's decision. Finally, the Council of Constantinople in 381 put the nails in the coffin of Apollinarianism. The primary defender of theological orthodoxy was Gregory of Nazianzus, a fourth-century Archbishop of Constantinople devoted to orthodox Trinitarian theology.

Gregory saw that Apollinarianism undermined the saving work of Jesus, which forced him to devote a vigorous letter-writing campaign against it. With laserlike precision, Gregory sliced through the error of sacrificing the full humanity of Jesus Christ. Salvation would be impossible under this heresy because "only a Christ who had all the elements of human nature could redeem all of man, and if every phase of man's nature were not redeemed, redemption would not be a fact."[10] What a tragedy it would be if the saving work of Christ only partially saved humanity! Gregory came up with a simple formula to summarize everything: "What has not been assumed has not been healed."[11] For Jesus Christ to be the full and appropriate mediator of the hostility between God and man, he himself had to be both fully God and fully man. The God-man.

To strengthen his argument, Gregory discussed Christ's role as the second Adam. He commented, "If anyone has put his trust in him as a man without a human mind, he is really bereft of mind, and quite unworthy of salvation. For that which he has not assumed he has not healed; but that which is united to his Godhead is also saved. If only half Adam fell, then that which Christ assumes and saves may be half also; but if the whole of his nature fell, it must be united to the whole nature of Him that was begotten, and so be saved as a whole."[12] In other words, if all of Adam was lost and ruined by the fall, then Christ, the second Adam, must put on all that Adam possessed in order to restore human nature and live the life that Adam failed to live.

Gregory stressed hard that the third aspect of humanity, the intellect, must be included in Christ's nature along with body and soul. Christ did not merely clothe himself with a human body; he was fully human with a functioning human mind as well. Gregory asked, "But if [Christ] has a soul, and yet is without a mind, how is He man, for man is not a mindless animal?"[13] The man Jesus Christ was a tabernacle in which the fully divine Son dwelled. If you take away the human mind of Christ, the Son might as well dwell in an "ox, or some other brute creatures."[14] So Gregory concluded that the logic of an Apollinarian description of the personhood of Christ is equally damaging to the doctrine of the Trinity. The orthodox doctrine of the Trinity taught that there are multiple (three) persons, but they all share one nature in the Godhead, preserving monotheism. Conversely, the personhood of Christ shares multiple (two) natures — God and man, timeless and subject to time, invisible and visible — yet he is one person.[15]

Contemporary Relevance

The insights of faithful churchmen such as Gregory of Nazianzus are important for us today as we consider the saving work of Jesus. If Apollinarius is right and the "Word" replaced the human mind of Jesus, we are left wondering how Christ can be fully human. The Gospels depict Jesus as being completely human in the way he experienced sorrow, pain, and other genuinely human experiences.[16] Certainly Jesus Christ was fully God, as the council of Nicaea maintained, but he was also fully man. And it was his deity as well as his humanity that allowed him to be our perfect substitute, the mediator between God and humanity for us and for our salvation.

An interesting way to evaluate the status of orthodox Christianity is to listen to the critiques of outsiders. For example, influential liberal New Testament scholar John A. T. Robinson (1919–83) lampooned orthodox Christians for their view of Christ. He believed that if you asked any typical Christian to describe the nature of Christ's birth or the personhood of Christ, one would most likely receive an answer that is essentially Apollinarianism. That is, "Christ only appeared to be a man or looked like a man: 'underneath' he was God." If they were pressed harder to talk about the humanity of Christ, they would most likely repudiate the idea that Christ was not a "perfect man" as well as "perfect God." However as a liberal who rejected any kind of supernaturalism, he further critiqued, "The traditional supranaturalistic way of describing the Incarnation almost inevitably suggests that Jesus was really God almighty walking about on earth, dressed up as a man. Jesus was not a man born and bred — he was God for a limited period taking part in a charade. He looked like a man, he talked like a man, he felt like a man, but underneath he was God dressed up — like Father Christmas. However guardedly it may be stated, the traditional view leaves the impression that God took a space-trip and arrived on this planet in the form of a man. Jesus was not really one of us; but through the miracle of the Virgin Birth he contrived to be born so as to appear one of us. Really he came from outside."[17]

If one can overlook the snide tone, Robinson's observation has merit. If not adequately taught, a typical orthodox Christian may imagine the incarnation in Apollinarian terms.

The evangelical tendency to overemphasize the divinity of

Christ at the expense of Christ's humanity came from overreacting to liberal doctrines in the nineteenth and twentieth centuries. Liberals called the church to abandon any kind of literal miracles to make Christianity more palpable to a modern society. Of course, on the one hand, biblical orthodoxy cannot embrace the liberal view that Jesus was only a man (John 1:1, 18). He was and is and always will be fully God. On the other hand, orthodoxy ought not be defined solely as a polar opposite of its opponent. This was the trap into which Apollinarius fell. Our beliefs must be biblical. Therefore, the full humanity of Christ is a crucial doctrine to be taught and believed, because he must be one of us in order to save us (Heb. 2:17 – 18).

Discussion Questions

1. Do you believe the Bible teaches that a human is made of three aspects: body, soul, and spirit? Or two aspects: body and soul (or material and immaterial)? Why?
2. Apollinarius taught that Jesus' divine nature/*Logos* replaced the human rational soul in the incarnation. What is lost if Jesus Christ is not fully human? How is salvation affected?
3. Do you agree with John A. T. Robinson's observation about the typical Christian's understanding of the nature of Jesus Christ?
4. What are some ways the church can make sure its new members — whether children or new converts — have a correct understanding of the nature of the incarnation?

Further Reading

Apollinaris of Laodicea. "On the Union in Christ of the Body with the Godhead." In *The Christological Controversies*. Edited and translated by Richard A. Norris Jr. Philadelphia: Fortress, 1980.

Daley, Brian. "'Heavenly Man' and 'Eternal Christ': Apollinarius and Gregory of Nyssa on the Personal Identity of the Savior." *Journal of Early Christian Studies* 10, no. 4 (Winter 2002): 469 – 88.

Gregory of Nazianzus. "Division I. Letters on the Apollinarian Controversy." In *Nicene and Post-Nicene Fathers: Second Series*. 10 vols. Edited by Philip Schaff and Henry Wace. Peabody, MA: Hendrickson, 1995.

Meredith, Anthony. *The Cappadocians*. Crestwood, NY: St. Vladimir's Seminary Press, 1997.

Raven, Charles Earle. *Apollinarianism: An Essay on the Christology of the Early Church*. Cambridge: Cambridge Univ. Press, 1923.

CHAPTER 9

PELAGIUS

God Has Already Given Us the Tools

Historical Background

Early in the fifth century, a controversy boiled over in the Western church about the origin of sin, the freedom of the will, and the nature of God's grace. Christians in the first four centuries held two beliefs concerning human nature:

1. Humanity is fallen and requires divine help for salvation.
2. Humans have a will and are responsible for their sin.

Just like the apparent paradox of the doctrine of the Trinity — God is one but exists in three persons — the two ideas were difficult to reconcile. The conflict came to a head with the clash of two popular teachers: Pelagius and Augustine.

Pelagius was a heretic of a different sort. He was Trinitarian and held to the divinity and humanity of Christ. This gave him the benefit of the doubt with many Christians at the time, but what landed him in trouble was his understanding of the fall of humanity. Understanding Pelagius's historical context is helpful here.

Pelagius was born around AD 350 in Britain. The details of his life are shrouded in mystery, but historians know he became a monk and eventually moved to Rome to teach the Bible. He had a mild personality, and there was no controversy surrounding his early life. However, upon seeing the lax moral discipline in Rome, he developed a reputation for being a spiritual director who urged people to reform their behavior and live lives as upstanding, moral citizens. It must be understood that Constantine had not only Christianized the Roman Empire in the fourth century but also brought about the "secularization" of the Christian church.[1] Before Christendom, as it came to be known, Christians were being persecuted or ignored. It was a serious choice to become one. After Christians gained considerable power in the Roman Empire, it became politically expedient to be a Christian. Nominal Christians increased in number as a result.[2]

To counter the dangerous moral laxity that he observed, Pelagius developed an ascetic form of Christianity with an optimistic theology of human nature. He pled for a sense of urgency about moral reformation and a pursuit of "real" Christianity. As historian Peter Brown notes, Pelagius lived in a world where Christians occupied more positions of power than they ever had before.[3] Out of his discussions with these sophisticated men, Pelagius formed the basis of his theology in his *Expositions of the Letters of St. Paul*.

Before 410, Pelagius had to flee Rome to avoid the invasion of the Arian Gothic leader Alaric.[4] He then moved to North Africa, where he met intense opposition, before migrating to Palestine. In 418 he was banished from Jerusalem, after which he vanished from the historical record. His teaching was condemned by the Council of Ephesus in 431.

Heretical Teaching

The starting point of Pelagius's moralistic theology was his insistence that God would never command anything that is impossible for humans to carry out. Pelagius emphasized humans' unconditional free will and moral responsibility. Specifically, Pelagius took issue with Augustine's prayer in his *Confessions*: "I have no hope at all but in your great mercy. Command what you will: give what you command."[5] He felt that this kind of talk encouraged laziness rather than piety, and that laziness is not a safe state of mind when it comes to sin.

Pelagius saw Augustine's prayer as turning humans into puppets determined by God's action. Indeed, he thought that God's commanding a person to do something that he lacked the ability to do would be useless: "To call a person to something he considers impossible does him no good."[6] If God called humans to live moral lives, Pelagius thought, it should be within their own power to carry out God's commands.

In his *Letter to Demetrias*, Pelagius laments that Christians do not consider it an honor to be ruled by God's precepts in his Word. He writes, "In fact, we act like lazy and insolent servants, talking back to our Lord in a contemptuous and slovenly way: 'That is too hard, too difficult! We cannot do that! We are only human; our flesh is weak!' What insane stupidity! What impious arrogance! We accuse the Lord of all knowledge of being doubly ignorant. We assert that he does not understand what he made and does not realize what he commands ... The just one did not choose to command the impossible; nor did the loving one plan to condemn a person for what he could not avoid."[7]

Notice Pelagius believed that God commands only according to our abilities. In Matthew 5:48, Jesus commands, "Be perfect, therefore, as your heavenly Father is perfect." Pelagius interpreted this to mean that perfection must be within our reach. Since perfection is achievable, it should therefore be obligatory.

It is important to understand that Pelagius's motivation was good. He saw one form of God's divine sovereignty as eliminating human responsibility. Moreover, Pelagius intended to avoid the error of the Manicheans (see chapter 5), who posited a dualism between immaterial good and material evil (and since Augustine had been a Manichaean before his conversion to Christianity, Pelagius was doubly suspicious of his emphasis on the evil of human nature). In the Manichaean view of humanity, to be human (even before Adam's fall from grace) is to be inherently evil, and the highest good is achieved in the soul's separation from the evil body. Pelagius, however, saw human nature as something good created by God.

It is the result of the fall upon humanity (original sin), however, that Pelagius ignores, causing his theology to fall into error. First, Pelagius argued that there is no such thing as original sin. In no way were humans after Adam guilty of or implicated in his first sin. Adam's sin in no way makes humans guilty or corrupt. Instead, "over the years [our own sin] gradually corrupts us, building an addiction and then holding us bound with what seems like the force of nature itself."[8] Humans by nature have a clean slate — a state of neutrality — according to Pelagius, and it is only through voluntary sin through the exercise of an unhampered human free will that humans are made wicked. Potentially, then, one could live a sinless life and merit heaven, for there is nothing intrinsically sinful about humans even after Adam and Eve's sin. Pelagius didn't consider humans to be intrinsically damnable after the fall.

In short, Pelagius rejected the doctrines of original sin, substitutionary atonement (the idea that Christ's death in our place is a supernatural intervention to save us), and justification by faith (the idea that believing and trusting in Christ is the way to salvation). This had major implications for Pelagius's theology of the freedom of the will, the origin of sin, and the nature of grace.

Pelagius on the Freedom of the Will

Early-church scholar J. N. D. Kelly observes that "the keystone of [Pelagius's] whole system is the idea of unconditional free will and responsibility."[9] Humans are given the unique privilege of carrying out God's will by their own choice. Pelagius identifies three elements in conduct: ability, will, and act. The first one comes from God, while the latter two are strictly humanity's. This means that God has given us all the tools we need to do good, but it is up to us to want to do good and to carry it out. Hence, people are responsible for their own sins and cannot blame any outside influences (addiction, abuse, duress, or most especially original sin). As seen in Pelagius's quote above, if we say we are incapable, we impugn God's creative ability. God made humans to be good.

Pelagius on the Origin of Sin

Most Christian theologians would reply, "Yes, but what about the fall?" Pelagius would reply that it had nothing to do with our sins. Yes, Adam was a bad example for his descendants, but his sins affected only himself. Pelagius rejected as absurd and unjust the doctrine Augustine termed "original sin." Why should a person be punished for another person's sins? The human duty to self-improvement could not be abandoned. People are born sinless, just like Adam. We sin not because we are born sinners but because we make a deliberate choice to do so. Sin exists only in the act. Pelagius taught that many Old Testament heroes were able to remain sinless, and since it had been done before, we are therefore without excuse.

Pelagius on the Nature of Grace

So what about grace? Pelagius did not discard grace entirely, but he did not understand it to mean dependance on God for salvation. When Pelagius spoke of grace, he meant the natural ability that God had given humanity to control their affairs, rather than a supernatural intervention. God has given us the grace to obey him. Pelagius also spoke in terms of instruction. It is by grace that we have the Word of God. So the grace of God through Jesus Christ is his perfect example of obedience.

According to Augustine, Pelagius's disciple Caelestius summarized Pelagianism succinctly with this list:

1. Adam was created mortal, and he would have died, whether he sinned or not.

2. Adam's sin injured himself alone, not the human race.
3. The law, as well as the gospel, leads to the kingdom.
4. There were men without sin before Christ's coming.
5. Newborn infants are in the same condition as Adam before the fall.
6. It is not through the death or the fall of Adam that the human race dies, nor through the resurrection of Christ that the whole human race rises again.[10]

Orthodox Response

Pelagius's teachings prompted a storm of anti-Pelagian literature, especially from the North African bishop Augustine, who opposed Pelagianism in many of his major works, such as *On the Spirit and the Letter* (412), *On Nature and Grace* (415), *On the Grace of Christ and on Original Sin* (418), *On Grace and Free Will* (427), and *On the Predestination of the Saints* (429).[11] Toward the end of his life, Augustine kept the sovereignty of God, human depravity, and humanity's need of grace at the center of his theology.

Augustine worked out his theology of humanity long before the Pelagian controversy. The amount of writings against Pelagius's view on the freedom of the will, origin of sin, and nature of grace showed how seriously Augustine considered Pelagius's errors to be.

Augustine on the Freedom of the Will

Augustine affirmed that humans were created with free will, teaching that only Adam and Eve had real freedom. This freedom was not in the fact that they had an inability to sin but rather because they had the ability not to sin. Pelagius said that humans started out in a neutral state but easily fell prey to bad habits. As the person commits more and more wrongs, he is less and less able to reform his life. Augustine said that after the fall, humans were preconditioned to commit wrong because Adam and Eve had sinned, and that all humans were guilty of that sin. The direction toward evil and away from God was already set. They are "not able not to sin." Hence, God must intervene and turn humans back toward him. Unlike Pelagius, who thought that hardened sinners are least likely to be able to return to God, Augustine believed that God sometimes chooses hardened sinners over the good, pious people in order to better show his grace.

Humans are restored after the mediation of divine grace in Jesus Christ through the work of the Holy Spirit — and only by the mediation of divine grace, for the will is bent in on itself and unable to choose to do good — and receive once again, by God's grace, the ability not to sin. Augustine writes, "This freedom of will is not therefore removed because it is assisted; it is assisted just because it is not removed. For he that says to God 'be thou my helper' confesses that He wills to fulfill what He has commanded, but that he asks the aid of Him who commanded that he may have power to fulfill it."[12] The range of freedom one enjoys is narrowed the deeper one is in sin, and broadened the deeper one is in Christ.

Augustine on the Origin of Sin

The problem is original sin. If Adam had not sinned, he would not have died.[13] But he did, so the consequences were severe. Augustine taught that the fall affected all of Adam's descendants with sin. Now every part of humankind is corrupted by sin, darkening the human mind and hardening the human heart. Furthermore, all human beings are born guilty of Adam's sin. In other words, people are not sinners because we sin; we sin because we are born sinners. Sin is like a hereditary disease passed down from one generation to the next. Augustine called humans a "lump of sin" incapable of saving themselves.[14] He "was happy to regard the church as a hospital where fallen humanity could recover and grow gradually in holiness through grace."[15]

Augustine on the Nature of Grace

In On the Grace of Christ, Augustine charges Pelagius with ignoring Philippians 2:12 – 13, which urges Christians to work out their own salvation with fear and trembling even though God is actually at work in them.[16] Augustine says, "Thus [Paul] did not say, 'God works in you to be able,' as though they had willing and working of themselves and had no need of God's help for these two. Instead he said, 'It is God who works in you both to will and to accomplish.'"[17] Put differently, "it is clear that [Pelagius] located this capacity [to will and to work] in nature itself" rather than in divine grace.[18] Or further, "The grace Pelagius acknowledges is God's showing and revealing what we ought to do, not giving and helping us to do it."[19]

To Augustine, grace is the only way to salvation. In On Nature and Grace Augustine argued that if it were possible for a person to live a perfectly righteous life and be saved without faith in Christ, as Pelagius alleged, then Christ "died in vain" (Gal. 2:21).[20]

Albert Outler beautifully summarizes Augustine's view of grace: "Grace, for Augustine, is God's freedom to act without any external necessity whatsoever — to act in love beyond human understanding or control; to act in creation, judgment, and redemption; to give his Son freely as Mediator and Redeemer; to endue the Church with the indwelling power and guidance of the Holy Spirit; to shape the destinies of all creation and the ends of the two human societies, the 'city of earth' and the 'city of God.' Grace is God's unmerited love and favor."[21] Augustine is famous for his play on the Latin words *gratis* (free) and *gratiae* (grace): "This grace, however, of Christ, without which neither infants nor adults can be saved, is not rendered for any merits, but is given gratis, on account of which it is also called grace."[22]

Contemporary Relevance

The theology of Augustine won against Pelagianism only formally at the Council of Carthage (418). Pelagianism refused to die and has continued to live on in various forms throughout church history. As theologian Robert Reymond opines, human beings are born "with Pelagian hearts,"[23] meaning all people are prone to attempt salvation through natural means from within ourselves, rather than through the supernatural means of relying on God's grace. Ask most people, "Why would you go to heaven?" and if the person believes in heaven, a safe bet is that the answer will be, "Because I've tried my best to be a good person." One arrives at this common answer because of a combination of three basic Pelagian concepts:

1. Freedom is defined as independence from God's sovereignty.
2. Original sin is rejected; we are all born good. Sin is only in the act of the will.
3. Grace as unmerited favor from God is rejected, ignored, or unknown.

The combination of these three results in personal morality as the basis for salvation.

But this must be rejected, as it is clear from Scripture that "[t]here is no one righteous, not even one; there is no one who understands; there is no one who seeks God" (Rom. 3:10–11). This is because of original sin, as Paul writes, for "just as sin entered the world through one man, and death through sin, and in this way death came to all people, because all sinned" (Rom. 5:12).

Christ came to set us free from the bondage of sin, from which we are unable to break free on our own (John 8:34–36). Paul said that we are free from righteousness, but that leads to death (Rom. 6:20–23). We are called to freedom (Gal. 5:1, 13), and true freedom is not being left to do what we please but acting in the way that God has always intended for us (Rom. 6:18). We either serve sin or we serve God.

The good news is that we are not left to our own devices to choose righteousness, but we are changed and empowered by God's grace to love and obey God more and more. That is one of the roles of our

Helper the Holy Spirit (John 14:16–17). One day those redeemed in Christ will enjoy ultimate freedom, when sin will no longer be an option.

Understanding Pelagius's error and Augustine's contribution to the doctrine of sin is monumentally important today. Ignoring, as Pelagius did, the consequences the fall of Adam has on every human can lead to diminishing the multifaceted work of Christ. Jesus not only bore our sins on the cross but lived a perfect life in obedience to the Father through the power of the Holy Spirit — the life that Adam failed to live — in order to restore fallen humans to their original state of grace through union with him. But God not only saves humans by grace; he also sustains them by grace. As Augustine put it, "God set the strong one free and permitted him to do what he chose; he guards the weak so that by his gift the saints unfailingly choose the good and unfailing refuse to abandon it."[24] Without understanding the magnitude of sin and the plight of humanity, the gracious work of Jesus for us and our salvation seems superfluous, at best. First Peter 1:18–19 says, "For you know that it was not with perishable things such as silver or gold that you were redeemed from the empty way of life handed down to you from your ancestors, but with the precious blood of Christ, a lamb without blemish or defect." It is for this reason that the work of Augustine in upholding the truth of Scripture in the fifth century is relevant for the church today.

Discussion Questions

1. What does freedom mean to you? In the new heaven and the new earth, where Satan, sin, and death are all done away with, is it really freedom not to have a choice to sin anymore?
2. What do you think about sin? In what ways have you seen the concept of sin minimized or downplayed? How does minimizing the concept of sin affect ones understanding of salvation?
3. What role does holiness play in the life of grace?
4. Who gets the credit for our salvation? Why?

Further Reading

Brown, Peter. *Augustine of Hippo: A Biography*. Berkley: Univ. of California Press, 2000.

Burns, J. Patout, ed. and trans. *Theological Anthropology*. Sources of Early Christian Thought. Philadelphia: Fortress, 1981.

Rees, B. R. *Pelagius: Life and Letters*. Woodbridge: Boydell, 1991.

Warfield, Benjamin B. "Augustine and the Pelagian Controversy." In *The Works of Benjamin B. Warfield*. Reprint. Grand Rapids, MI: Baker, 2003.

CHAPTER 10

EUTYCHES

Christ as a New Kind of Being

Historical Background

If there is one word to describe the Eutychianist controversy, it would most certainly be "drama." The theological wars from the First Council of Nicaea (325) to the First Council of Constantinople (381) mostly dealt with how God the Father relates with God the Son. Once the doctrine of the Trinity was settled, the debate shifted to how the church should understand the person of the God-man, Jesus Christ. The councils of Nicaea and Constantinople already confessed him to be truly human and truly divine. But the remaining question was, How do Christ's two natures relate to one another in the incarnation?

Two great city centers dominated the discussion in a great theological tug-of-war. The city of Alexandria pulled hard to emphasize the unity of Christ's two natures. The city of Antioch pulled back with equal force, arguing that Jesus Christ's human and divine natures must maintain their distinction. Nestorius, Bishop of Constantinople, went too far with the Antiochene emphasis. He refused to acknowledge sufficient unity between Christ's two natures. They were to stay separate, making Christ seem like two persons. Cyril, Bishop of Alexandria, was appalled by this and wrote to Leo the

Great, Bishop of Rome, to join him in calling a third ecumenical council — the Council of Ephesus (431) — to condemn Nestorius (see chapter 11).

Much to the Alexandrians' dismay, Cyril reluctantly made a compromise with the school of Antioch by allowing talks of two natures of Christ. But Cyril clarified, "A distinction of the natures is necessary, a division is reprehensible."[1] Still, most historians agree the problem with Cyril's doctrine of Christ is that it was too ambiguous. He favored the formula "One nature after the union." This left the door wide open for future heresies such as Eutychianism.

The Council of Ephesus was only a temporary solution for both schools of thought. Cyril of Alexandria was satisfied because Nestorianism was condemned. Antiochene theologians were pleased that it was still necessary to acknowledge two distinct natures of Christ. But as historian Roger Olson puts it, "The council that was supposed to resolve the dispute and establish universal orthodoxy ... opened up a greater conflict and forced another council to bring it to closure."[2] A fourth ecumenical council was inevitable.

Until the Council of Chalcedon, the atmosphere in the Mediterranean seemed to be the calm before the storm. There was no complete agreement, but at least there was peace and fellowship between the bishops of Alexandria, Antioch, Constantinople, and Rome — the four most powerful bishops, known as the patriarchs. But it was an uneasy peace, and a new patriarch soon upset the balance.

Cyril died in 444, leaving Dioscorus — a man with some serious character flaws — to succeed him as bishop of Alexandria. More than seeking to renew the doctrinal war between Alexandria and Antioch, Dioscorus sought "to advance the Alexandrian see to the supremacy of the entire East."[3] At the time, the current bishop of Constantinople favored the Antiochene school, so the goal was to undo that partnership. Constantinople was the prize. It was strategic to win over the capital city of the eastern Roman Empire to exert influence on the rest of the churches. Then Dioscorus might be able to obliterate any talk of two natures of Christ, because he sincerely believed it inevitably led to Nestorianism.

The drama began to build up in the capital city of the eastern Roman Empire. Theologian Theodoret of Cyrus was most likely on his way to become the next bishop of Constantinople. He was also the favored son of Antioch. Clearly, Dioscorus did not like this one bit. So he schemed privately and an incidental controversy provided a solution for him. Rather than poking at the house of cards himself, Dioscorus allowed someone else to do it unwittingly for him — Eutyches (378–454).

Heretical Teaching

Despite the fact that the heresy bears Eutyches' name, he was mostly a pawn in the whole controversy. Nothing is known about his life except that he was an elderly monk of Constantinople. He spent most of his later life in seclusion as an archimandrite (head of a cloister of three hundred monks). The only time he raised his head in public was at the Council of Ephesus to condemn Nestorius, but he quickly retreated into seclusion to teach thereafter.

Whereas the heretic Nestorius was guilty of overemphasizing the distinct natures of Christ and thereby positing two persons (one human and one divine), Eutyches was guilty of so emphasizing the unity of the one person that he blurred the distinction between the divine and human natures.

As a radical Alexandrian, he denied that theologians should talk about two natures after the incarnation. This, however, was not what got him into trouble. Alexandrians had been arguing this for a long time. The teaching that triggered a controversy afresh was his denial that Christ shared the same substance, or essence, with humankind. To Eutyches, the human nature and divine nature both assimilated in Christ, resulting in a single new nature — a third kind of nature, in which categories were blurred. An appropriate analogy is that Christ's humanity was like "a drop of wine in the ocean of his deity" — the ocean was now part wine rather than purely water, but only a very small part.[4] About Eutyches, Stephen Nichols writes, "To him Christ was a third thing (the Latin expression is *tertium quid*).... One new and different person fashioned out of two natures is how he liked to put it. That is a theological way of saying yellow and blue makes green."[5]

Theodoret made Eutychian theology known more widely in 447 by writing *Eranistes*, a three-part theological dialogue between "Orthodoxos" and "Eranistes" (beggar).[6] Orthodoxos represented Theodoret's thought, and though he never mentioned Eutyches by name, Eranistes was a supporter of Eutychianism. In the third dialogue, Theodoret clearly placed Eutyches' teaching in a category with Alexander the coppersmith (2 Tim. 4:14), Valentinus, Apollinarius, and Arius — he called it a heresy.[7]

Dioscorus used this book as an opportunity to shake up the relative peace between the schools of Alexandria and Antioch. He manipulated a court in Constantinople to take action against Eutyches in 448 and at the same time he accused Theodoret of Nestorianism. Eutyches was forced to defend himself. Theodoret and Domnus, bishop of Antioch, likewise came to defend their own views. Eutyches admitted that "the holy Virgin" had the same substance as us, but skirted around admitting whether the Son did as well. When pressed about whether he believed there were two natures in Christ, Eutyches suggested that there was only one nature in Christ after the incarnation, and insisted he simply followed Athanasius and Cyril: "I admit that our Lord was of two natures before the union, but after the union one nature.... I follow the doctrine of the blessed Cyril and the holy fathers and the holy Athanasius. They speak of two natures before the union, but after the union and incarnation they speak of one nature not two."[8] However, the extent to which Eutyches' position stands in continuity with that of Athanasius and Cyril is questionable, at best. When all was heard, the local synod charged Eutyches with error and deposed him of his position. Theodoret and Domnus were acquitted of their charges.

Now there was a propaganda war from both sides trying to persuade distant bishops to come to their side. Eutyches went on to appeal to Leo the Great for refuge.[9] At the same time, Dioscorus swayed Emperor Theodosius II to support Eutyches, as well. Just when Dioscorus thought he had completed his scheme, Leo threw a wrench into his plan with a letter to Flavian, Bishop of Constantinople. Leo confirmed the synod's decision and gave sophisticated reasonings for his condemnation of Eutyches' theology of Christ. This famous letter came to be known as Leo's "Tome."[10] Eutyches eventually found refuge in Alexandria with Dioscorus.

The emperor called a second council in Ephesus (449) to resume peace, but it became one of the biggest scandals in church history. One hundred and thirty-five bishops showed up, but Theodoret was not invited. Dioscorus arrived with an intimidating entourage of thuggish monks, essentially silencing Flavian and his friends. Flavian had no chance to read Leo's Tome. One representative, however, spoke in favor of two natures of Christ, but he was shouted down by many: "Let (him) be burnt; let him be burnt alive. As he has cut Christ in two, so let him be cut in two."[11] Representatives of Leo saw the writing on the wall, so they departed early to avoid being identified with the council. In the final decision, the council condemned a theology of two natures of Christ as heresy and excommunicated its advocates: Theodoret, Flavian, and Leo. Eutyches' theology of only one new nature of Christ was reaffirmed and he was restored to his former position.

Dioscorus succeeded in his scheme. With the backing of the emperor and a so-called ecumenical council in his pocket, he felt justified to send his aggressive monks to attack Flavian when he sought to convene another council to counteract the Second Council of Ephesus. Flavian died as a result, leaving Anatolius, a friend of Dioscorus, to become the next patriarch of Constantinople. It now seemed the whole Eastern church was subjugated to the Eutychian doctrine of Christ, but things worked out differently than Dioscorus planned.

Orthodox Response

Leo of Rome would not go down without a fight. Horrified with the recent decisions and events, he famously dubbed the second council in Ephesus "the Robber Synod." He appealed to Emperor Theodosius to reverse all the decisions in the council and to arrest the murderers of Flavian. Not surprisingly, Theodosius refused all of Leo's demands. Leo then began the process of calling another ecumenical council to meet in the West without the emperor's approval. By this time, relations between the East and the West were so distant in the Roman Empire, he knew he did not have to worry about any retaliation from the emperor.

But in the following year (450), Leo's fight against the East became unnecessary. Theodosius died in a freak accident, having been thrown off his horse. Dioscorus's main source of political power to uphold his heresy in the East was now suddenly removed.

To add further problems for Eutychianism, Theodosius's successor — his sister Pulcheria and her husband, Marcian — advocated for the capital city to be completely independent from too much alliance with either schools of Alexandria or Antioch. They ordered Flavian's body to be returned to Constantinople so that he might be buried with full honors. Then they called a fourth ecumenical council to replace Ephesus II (the Robber Synod) and meet at Chalcedon. The anti-Eutychian letter, Leo's Tome, was distributed to the five hundred bishops ordered to attend. It was fairly obvious to Dioscorus that the Council of Chalcedon was not going his way, but he nevertheless went to the council with a fighting spirit, calling for the excommunication of Leo.

The tension between the schools of Alexandria and Antioch was high.[12] Yet the Council of Chalcedon also sought to bridge the two schools by avoiding the extremities of either party and upholding respective truths they both guarded. A new statement of orthodox belief about the person of Jesus Christ was very much needed, but the council was clear that the formulation of Chalcedon was not a new creed but an interpretation and elaboration of the Nicene Creed of 381.

Leo's Tome proved to be a persuasive argument for the necessity of distinguishing two natures of Christ. Leo declared in it, "For He who is true God is also true man: and in this union there is no lie, since the humility of manhood and the loftiness of the Godhead both meet there. For God is not changed by the showing of pity, so man is not swallowed up by the dignity. For each form does what is proper to it with the co-operation of the other ..."[13] Notice that in the first statement, Leo restates the Nicene declaration that Christ is both truly God and truly man. The human nature and the divine nature in Christ remain distinct and unmixed in the incarnation so that Jesus is truly God and truly man. Because Eutyches denied this by teaching that Christ's humanity is swallowed up in his divinity, Leo accused him of teaching another form of Docetism, thus the statement "there is no lie."[14]

On the other side of the same coin, Cyril's letter to Nestorius and another one to John of Antioch were discussed at the council to emphasize the single personhood of Christ. In the latter letter, Cyril acknowledged to John, "we confess that our Lord Jesus Christ ... is complete God and complete human being with a rational soul and body ... This same one is coessential (of the same being) with the Father, as to his deity, and coessential with us, as to his humanity, for a union of two natures has occurred, as a consequence of which we confess one Christ, one Son, one Lord."[15] Though Cyril acknowledged Christ's two natures, he emphasized that we must confess Christ as one Lord without confusion.

In the end, the council recognized that Jesus Christ is one person who exists with two distinguishable natures. To make this clearer and to avoid future heresies, the council crafted "the Definition of Chalcedon." Four fences were constructed around the mystery of the person of Christ — namely, he is "recognized in two natures, without confusion, without change, without division, without separation." The definition went on to say that "the distinction of natures" was in no way "annulled by the union, but rather the characteristics of each nature being preserved and coming together to form one person and subsistence."[16] This definition made sure to exclude Eutychianism and Nestorianism from any place in orthodox Christianity.[17]

Contemporary Relevance

The political scheming in the Eutychian controversy is off-putting; however, the orthodox doctrine of the person of Christ is crucial for followers of Christ. The bishops at Chalcedon labored hard to craft a careful statement that distinguished the two natures in one person because salvation depends on both natures of Christ. Stephen Nichols puts the problem with Eutychianism this way: "The problem with stressing the unity without the counterbalance of the two intact natures, as Eutyches does, is that Christ loses his human and divine identity. As such, he is not truly our representative. The Christ of Eutyches falls way short of Paul's teaching of Christ as the last Adam (Rom. 5:12–21; 1 Cor. 15:42–49)."[18]

This is the problem Leo the Great identified, and it was the problem with all the christological heresies in the early church. The orthodox theologians of the first several centuries saw an intimate connection between the incarnation and the atoning work of Christ. Thus Leo writes, "Without detriment therefore to the properties of either substance which then came together in one person, majesty took on humility, strength weakness, eternity mortality; and for the paying off of the debt belonging to our condition, inviolable nature was united with passible nature, and true God and true man were combined to form one Lord, so that, as suits the needs of our case, one and the same Mediator between God and man, the man Christ Jesus, could both die with the one and rise again with the other."[19]

In Leo's view, it is the fact that Christ became human, even including the awkward or embarrassing parts of humanity, that allows him to advocate for us in our own weakness and sinfulness.

Eutyches' attempt to honor Christ by downplaying his humanity took away the purpose of his mission.

Discussion Questions

1. One of the results of a Eutychian view of Jesus Christ is that his humanity becomes overwhelmed and enveloped by his divinity. How does this view that even Jesus' humanity is in some way divine make it difficult to think of Christ as a human being just like us?

2. The orthodox response to Eutychianism was to develop a robust understanding of both the divinity and the humanity of Jesus Christ. In what ways do the Old Testament prophecies about Jesus Christ require that he be both human and divine? What New Testament passages teach clearly Jesus' divinity? What passages teach about his humanity?

3. Because Jesus' humanity was not blended with his divinity like Eutyches taught, it was like our humanity in every way (except sin). Are there any places in the New Testament that show the Holy Spirit ministering to Jesus in the same way the Holy Spirit ministers to us?

Further Readings

Grillmeier, Aloys, S.J. *Christ in Christian Tradition*, vol. 1, *From the Apostolic Age to Chalcedon (451)*. Translated by John Bowden. Atlanta: John Knox, 1975.

Norris, Richard A., trans. and ed. *The Christological Controversy*. Sources of Early Christian Thought. Philadelphia: Fortress, 1980.

CHAPTER 11

NESTORIUS

Christ's Divinity Must Be Shielded

Historical Background

The period of controversy surrounding Nestorius in the early fifth century is one of the most important periods of christological discussion in the history of the church. The orthodox position had always been that Christ was both God and man, and the Council of Nicaea, in 325, had codified this position: "We believe in one Lord, Jesus Christ, the only Son of God, eternally begotten of the Father, God from God, Light from Light, true God from true God, begotten, not made, of one Being with the Father. Through him all things were made. For us and for our salvation he came down from heaven: by the power of the Holy Spirit he became incarnate from the Virgin Mary, and was made man."

But it was one thing merely to say that Jesus was both God and man; since he was a historical person, what did that mean? How much God was he, and how much man? Did it mean that he had two minds — a divine and a human one — which seems impossible, or did it mean that the divine part of him overwhelmed the human part, which seems to contradict the idea that he was fully human?

As the fifth-century church wrestled with how to understand how Jesus could be both God and man, two main theological "schools" competed: the Alexandrian school and the Antiochene school.[1] The Alexandrians tended to focus on Jesus' deity and the unity of the divine *Logos* with the human person of Jesus, and their chief proponent, Cyril the Patriarch of Alexandria (ca. 348–444), described the identity of Christ as a "hypostatic union" of God and man into one *prosopon*, or person.[2] The Antiochene school, on the other hand, favored a historical, literal approach that emphasized the humanity of Jesus; they believed the completeness of both the divine and human natures of Christ to be paramount. Their concern was driven by the belief that salvation is possible only because the Son of God became completely human; as fourth-century theologian Gregory of Nazianzus put it, "That which was not assumed, was not healed."[3] This emphasis led to a distinction between the infinite Godhead and the finite humanity in the person of Christ. Both schools tended to be misunderstood by the other side. The Antiochene position tended to be misconceived as teaching that Christ was two persons, while the Alexandrian emphasis drew accusations of Monophysitism, the heresy that Jesus had one merged divine-human nature.[4]

Out of the Antiochene stream of thought came Nestorius (ca. 386–451), who was appointed Patriarch of Constantinople in June of 428. Fervent, stubborn, and politically naive, he quickly alienated many of the people in the city. For instance, after assuring the emperor, Theodosius II, that the empire would triumph over its enemies once the emperor threw out all heretics, Nestorius proceeded to burn down a chapel belonging to members of the Arian heresy.[5] A great deal of the city also burned as a result of the fire, which earned Nestorius the nickname "Torchie."[6] In another instance, Nestorius refused a request by the Roman pope, Celestine, to return some Pelagian heretics who were taking refuge in Constantinople.[7] Nor did he show himself open to listening to other points of view — when he could not answer the questions of some monks during one of his sermons, he invited them to come to his house the following day to discuss the matter further; when the monks arrived, however, they were beaten by Nestorius's guards.[8] In a short time, Nestorius had made an impressive number of enemies, although he had enough friends among the nobility to ensure his continued reign as patriarch.

Heretical Teaching

Nestorius came to the center of theological controversy when he was asked to comment on whether it is fitting to call Jesus' mother Mary *Theotokos* ("Mother of God"). For Nestorius, who wanted to keep the two natures of Christ separate, this was a difficult assertion to make. While he maintained that Mary did indeed give birth to Christ, Nestorius thought it was inappropriate to speak of Mary as being the mother of God when she bore the child Jesus. God is eternal, and any attempt to say that God was born of Mary seemed to Nestorius to be closet Arianism (which taught that there was a time when the Son of God did not exist). He said he could affirm *Theotokos* if *Anthropotokos* ("Mother of Man"; together, "Mother of the God-Man") was added to her title. He considered *Christotokos* ("Mother of Christ") the most fitting title, for as J. N. D. Kelly notes, "God cannot have a mother, [Nestorius] argued, and no creature could have engendered the Godhead. Mary bore a man, the vehicle of divinity but not God."[9]

Nestorius maintained that Jesus Christ not only had two natures, divine and human, but that in the incarnation, he maintained two distinct persons, and that these two persons and natures could not be mixed or confused. Following the Nicene Creed, he maintained that Jesus Christ shared a full nature with God and a full nature with humankind. "Person" is a harder concept, but in simple terms it is an acting subject or consciousness. When the Nicene Creed used the word "consubstantial" (of the same substance), it was talking about nature; Jesus had the same nature as the Father. For Nestorius, Jesus Christ had and maintained two natures and two persons. At no time did the nature of the *Logos* mix with the nature of the man Jesus. The persons also remained distinct: a person of the *Logos* and a person of the man Jesus. This distinction was important for several reasons. First, it seemed to explain why the gospel writers describe Jesus as being ignorant of events which God would have to know because he is omniscient. Second, it also protected the "impassibility" of God. In the Greek mind, God is unable to change, because change implies that something is less than perfect, that it can be improved in some way. It was believed that God cannot suffer[10] because God cannot change. And therefore, because Christ was fully God, he was not able to suffer. But Jesus obviously suffered during the events of Good Friday. Nestorius's solution was that the natures and the persons remained distinct. The human person of Jesus Christ suffered, but the divine person of Jesus Christ did not.

Nestorius acknowledged he developed his Christology in the light of the major heresies of Arianism and Manichaeanism.[11] Nestorius attempted to form a Christology that upheld orthodox Christian teachings against these two heresies and others like it. Against the Arians, who mingled the human and divine parts of Jesus, Nestorius held firmly to the belief that Jesus was both fully God and fully man, and that these parts were separate. Thus, Jesus could really suffer for the redemption of humankind, in his passible, human part, but remain in control and impassible in his divine part.[12] Against the Manichaeans, who believed that a human Christ would actually be a detriment to salvation, Nestorius tended to emphasize that Jesus was fully human in all points. That Jesus was human in every possible way was crucial to the way that Nestorius conceived of the atonement — in his body, Jesus was a substitute for those who were like himself, so that they would be able to pass through death into the resurrected life. "And since many are brought low by the fear of death," Nestorius wrote, "he endured unto death and gave a just compensation for us in that he exchanged for our death the death which came unjustly upon him."[13] If Jesus were somehow not like us, his atonement would be invalid.[14]

Nestorius wanted to reject any sort of suffering in the divine nature of Christ while insisting that Christ also grew and was tempted. On the other hand, he wanted to maintain that Christ really was divine. The two-person model seemed the best way to do that. In his mind the separation of the natures of Christ and the emphasis on Christ's humanity did not mean that Jesus was two separate people or that he was not fully God.[15] Although his opponents often accused him of holding such positions, it is important to understand that Nestorius himself did not believe that he had overstepped any boundaries.

Orthodox Response

The chief opponent of Nestorius was Cyril (ca. 376–444), Patriarch of Alexandria from 412 to 444. Like Nestorius, Cyril had also earned a less than stellar reputation for being antagonistic. His tenure as Patriarch of Alexandria saw the murder of a female pagan philosopher,[16] as well as the breakdown of secular Roman authority in favor of rule by militant monks.[17] Unlike Nestorius, however, he had twenty-five years of political experience by the time of the council and is generally considered a deeper thinker and a more profound theologian than his rival.

Where Nestorius emphasized the humanity of Jesus as crucial for salvation, Cyril believed that the real importance lay in the divinity of Jesus. What Cyril found most troubling about Nestorius's two-nature theory was that the humanity of Jesus could potentially be so opaque that the divinity of Jesus would not be able to shine through. Cyril argued that if Jesus had two natures, one God and one man, and if to everyone around him he seemed to be like every other man, then he could offer no more salvation than Moses could. Those who worshiped Jesus would worship only the outward, human form[18] and those who were reshaped in his image would only be reshaped to resemble his human nature.[19] For Cyril, Nestorius's theory threatened the idea of Jesus as the "express image of God" and "God among us."

Furthermore, Cyril thought that Nestorius's theology threatened the unity of Jesus and ultimately made Jesus into two people who were loosely tied together. He was just as concerned as Nestorius with establishing Jesus as a human being rather than a God who was cloaked in humanity, but he thought that if Christ suffered only in his human form, he would not be an effective high priest.[20] Cyril held that it was through *divine* suffering that Christ mediated the sins of humankind, and so even though the suffering of God on the cross might be a paradox, it is nevertheless a nonnegotiable principle of the faith.

For Cyril, it was proper to call Mary the "Mother of God" because in the incarnation, the nature of the *Logos* was united with the nature of humankind in the single person of Jesus Christ. Since Christ was a single person, it was proper to use the term that belongs to either nature to refer to the single person Jesus Christ. This is called the *communicatio idiomatum*, or communication of properties.[21] The communication of properties means you can say that God suffered on the cross, or that the baby Jesus lying in the manger was the creator of the heavens and the earth — because it is hard to wrap your mind around two such opposite images, the communication of properties reminds us that it is sufficient just to think of one at a time, with the understanding that both are equally true.

In 429, Cyril heard that Nestorius refused to recognize Mary as *Theotokos*, and the two exchanged a series of heated letters. Cyril wrote to Pope Celestine with a summary of Nestorius's views, asking him to pass judgment on whether Nestorius was truly teaching the faith of Nicaea. Cyril's motives were not purely doctrinal. He hoped to embarrass Constantinople, because the authorities there wanted to claim ecclesiastical jurisdiction second only to Rome, and Cyril considered their efforts a purely political move and not grounded in the history of the church. If the Bishop of Constantinople were declared a heretic, perhaps this would lessen the threat of Constantinople. Cyril and Nestorius both appealed to Pope Celestine, but he sided with Cyril and held a synod in Rome (430) to affirm the title

Theotokos against Nestorius. Cyril informed Nestorius of the ruling and ordered him to cease his teaching and recant his position; he wrote a long letter to Nestorius consisting of twelve anathemas that were "deliberately provocative."[22] It is likely that Cyril's new statement of anathemas was unfair, as it represented a more extreme version of Alexandrian Christology, which even moderate Antiochenes would have labeled Apollinarian. Consequently, Theodosius the emperor called a meeting in June of 431 at Ephesus. This meeting, later known as the First Council of Ephesus, was the climax of the conflict between Cyril and Nestorius.

It was perhaps inevitable that Cyril and Nestorius would clash over both politics and theology, considering they were representatives of rival theological schools (Alexandrian and Antiochene). When battle lines were drawn at the Council of Ephesus, the bishops largely split along ethnic lines — Syrians supported Nestorius, while Egyptians, Greeks, and Romans (whom Nestorius had alienated) backed Cyril.

The political background to the council can seem jarring to modern readers. It is useful to remember that the ancient world operated under different conceptions than we do. For instance, both Nestorius and Cyril believed that it was vital for the empire to hold the proper ideas about Christ in order for its people to prosper. Both were placed in a situation in which they were expected to forge political connections and wield authority, even authority that required the use of force. These circumstances might not excuse the actions that they undertook to win the council, but it must be understood that they were not simply power-hungry fanatics. However, both patriarchs were deeply concerned with understanding the nature of Christ in a way that was true to Scripture and that would lead others to salvation.

From the beginning, however, the Council of Ephesus was slanted in Cyril's favor. Although the council had been slated to take place at Constantinople, Pulcheria, the emperor's sister, moved it to Ephesus.[23] Pulcheria was a longtime enemy of Nestorius and knew that Ephesus was the site of a thriving shrine to Mary. The locals at Ephesus obviously favored the title of *Theotokos*, and their opinions became a key factor in the debate. Through a series of politically motivated and orchestrated events, few of the supporters of Nestorius arrived in time for the council, and Cyril and his supporters began the Council of Ephesus without them, amid some protest.

In an unfortunate blunder, Nestorius said that he refused to worship a God who was a baby of two or three months old.[24] By this he meant that if Mary were the mother of God, then it was implied that she was the mother of God in all his fullness — an obvious absurdity. The Cyrilline party took this statement as an opportunity to paint Nestorius as a heretic. They accused him of believing that Christ was a man whom God later made divine (the "adoptionist" heresy), a charge that was made more credible by the fact that Nestorius's home city of Antioch had produced a prominent adoptionist not long before named Paul of Samosata. The people of Ephesus either believed the charge of Adoptionism or used it as an excuse for their own ill will toward Nestorius, because threats were soon made against bishops friendly to Nestorius and several abandoned him for Cyril's side.[25]

The council decided against Nestorius and deposed him from his position as patriarch for his heretical views. As the council was wrapping up, Nestorius's supporters finally arrived and started their own council. This council met and deposed Cyril, restored Nestorius, and declared the previous council invalid. When the representatives from the pope finally arrived, they declared that Cyril and the council he led were the official council and Nestorius's view of two persons was condemned. In addition, the term *Theotokos* was officially approved. Mary was indeed to be called the Mother of God. Nestorius was stripped of his power and rank and driven into exile.

The council resulted in schism between the church of Antioch, which stood by Nestorius, and the church of Alexandria. In the years following the Council of Ephesus, however, the two sides reached a compromise with the Formula of Union in 433.[26] Concessions were made to the Diphysite (two-nature) Antiochene position, and the standard orthodox Christology formulated not long after at the Council of Chalcedon (451) settled that Christ had two natures united in one person, but the condemnation of Nestorius remained; he was deposed from his ecclesiastical position and eventually died in exile around 451.[27] The proposition that Jesus Christ contained in himself two distinct persons, God and man, was condemned as the heresy of "Nestorianism," though Nestorius himself vehemently rejected this description of his teaching and maintained his orthodoxy to the end.[28] However, the heresy of "two Sons" has remained associated with his name throughout the history of the Christian church.

Sympathizers of Nestorius fled the empire to Mesopotamia and Persia, where they established themselves in Nisibis, the intellectual center of the Persian church. The Persian church continued to honor Nestorius and eventually separated itself from the West when the Persian Empire began to clash with the eastern Roman Empire. In the next few centuries, Nestorian missionaries planted churches in Iran, India, Central Asia, and up to the coast of China.[29] Some of these communities survive to the present day. Inadvertently, the decision at Ephesus resulted in the expansion of Christianity; without the seemingly harsh ruling of the council, there would have been much less incentive to bring the gospel to those new territories.

Contemporary Relevance

The Nestorian controversy represents an important development in Christian theology. Despite their rivalry, both sides were seriously trying to understand how Christ saves humankind, and the questions they raised are worth deep consideration. How human was Christ? Did his humanity dilute or mask his divinity? Did his divinity interfere with the effectiveness of his sacrifice? As we have seen, the Council of Ephesus firmly promoted the unity of Christ's being, and despite the political wrangling, it did so because it considered

Nestorius's Christology as the beginning of a slippery slope that might disconnect Christ from his divinity in all but name. Later, the Council of Chalcedon (451) revisited the issue and moderated the decision made at Ephesus in a way that resolved some of Nestorius's concerns. But by taking a decisive stand for the unity of Christ's nature, the church had moved one step closer to a more articulate Christology that helped believers understand the work of salvation.

All of these questions may seem abstract and even irrelevant today, but they continue to have real implications for the way Christians see the life and ministry of Jesus. To take only one scenario, think of how differently we might interpret his temptation in the desert if we believed Jesus had a divine but not a human mind. Or consider his redemptive sufferings on the cross — what if he were suffering only as an ordinary human being, or conversely only as a human body propelled by a divine control center? Would that change how we look to Christ for salvation? These questions greatly concerned ancient theologians, and because the church wrestled through them in the fifth century, we have a clearer understanding of who Jesus is and how his life, death, and resurrection brought salvation to humanity.

Discussion Questions

1. Why was Nestorius so concerned with maintaining the distinction between Christ's divine and human natures? Why was Cyril so adamant about their unity?
2. How does the unity of Christ's natures affect the way we worship Christ?
3. How was the question of calling Mary *Theotokos* relevant to the nature of Christ?
4. What can the Nestorian controversy teach us today about the right and wrong ways to approach theological debates and disagreements?

Further Reading

Clayton, Paul B., Jr. *The Christology of Theodoret of Cyrus: Antiochene Christology from the Council of Ephesus (431) to the Council of Chalcedon (451)*. Oxford Early Christian Studies. Oxford: Oxford Univ. Press, 2007.

Cyril of Alexandria. *Five Tomes against Nestorius*. Oxford: James Parker, 1881.

Grillmeier, Aloys. *Christ in the Christian Tradition*. Vol. 2, *From the Council of Chalcedon (451) to Gregory the Great (590 – 604)*. Louisville: Westminster John Knox, 1995.

McGuckin, John. *St. Cyril of Alexandria and the Christological Controversy*. Crestwood, NY: St. Vladimir's Seminary Press, 2004.

Nestorius. *The Bazaar of Heracleides*. Translated by G. R. Driver and Leonard Hodgson. Oxford: Clarendon, 1925.

Wessel, Susan. *Cyril of Alexandria and the Nestorian Controversy: The Making of a Saint and of a Heretic*. Oxford Early Christian Studies. Oxford: Oxford Univ. Press, 2004.

CHAPTER 12

SOCINUS

The Trinity Is Irrelevant and Jesus' Death Is Only an Example

Historical Background

Faustus Socinus (1539–1604), also known as Fausto Sozzini or Faust Socyn, was born into a noble family of bankers and jurists and became independent early in life thanks to an inheritance he received from his grandfather. With independent wealth, Socinus chose various paths for study, showing promise in law and writing. Eventually, however, this Renaissance man with connections to the Sienese intellectual elite became famous for his theological thought. However, in orthodox circles, the fame that Socinus gained is not generally praiseworthy.

Though little is known of Socinus's childhood, by 1558, two of his uncles, Celso and Camillo, were suspected of Lutheranism, and they were pursued by the Catholic Inquisition. Another uncle, Lelio, had shifted his own studies from law to divinity and, in large part because of his family's money, had made acquaintances with some of the leading Reformers of the day, including Philip Melanchthon, John Calvin, and Heinrich Bullinger. During the 1550s, Lelio spent a considerable amount of time traveling throughout Europe seeking to gain access to his inheritance, which had been commandeered by the leaders of the Inquisition. Those travels eventually took him to Poland, where he became closely acquainted with several men who later led the anti-Trinitarian movement that gained traction in Poland.

Largely because of his family's reputation, Socinus came under the suspicion of the Inquisition as well, and, by 1559, he had fled with Lelio to Zurich for refuge. When Lelio died in 1562, Socinus acquired his uncle's papers (most of which were unpublished) and began his own writing career. After returning for a time to lands controlled by the Catholic Inquisition, Socinus finally fled to Transylvania and eventually to Poland, where he lived the remainder of his days.

In Polish lands, Socinus found not only a tolerance for religious diversity but also a community eager for his unorthodox teaching, which had already gained some notoriety for its anti-Trinitarian leanings, and he quickly gained influence in the Minor Reformed Church, or the Polish Brethren, a sect of the Protestant church in Poland that had separated from the Polish Reformed Church in 1565 over differences in their understanding of the doctrine of the Trinity.

Heretical Teaching

Beginning with his first publication in 1562, a work titled *An Explanation of the Prologue of the Book of the Gospel of John*, Socinus developed his understanding of the unity (rather than trinity) of the Godhead with Jesus' role as the divine *Logos* (usually translated "Word") being an office he held rather than an aspect of his nature. According to this view, only God the Father is truly and fully divine. Jesus, "the Son of God," received a unique divinely appointed office as the *Logos*, an office which deserves respect and even worship. However, for Jesus, that respect and worship were limited to his office and did not extend to his person, which Socinus argued was not divine. Two additional works, *Jesus Christ Savior* and *The State of Man before the Fall*, provided Socinus the opportunity to develop his theology into a full-fledged system built not only on his unitarian view of God but also on distinctive views of the atonement and the role of human reason. Socinus's church officially endorsed his teachings at the Synod of Racovia in 1603. Socinus died shortly thereafter, but the Racovian Academy, a school which had been established in 1602, began printing and disseminating Socinus's works, including his last and most influential work, a catechism known as the Racovian Catechism. The theological system held by Socinus affected every theological tenet, such that virtually no teaching held by the Socinians could be considered really orthodox.

Human Reason

The preeminent presupposition of the Socinian theological system was an elevation of individual human reason over and against church tradition and the divinely inspired revelation of God in Scripture. According to several acquaintances, Socinus emphatically declared that his only instructors had been his uncle, Lelio, and the Bible. Such lack of education, Socinus thought, did not compromise his theological capabilities. Instead, it safeguarded him against the errant teachings of human traditions, allowing him to perceive the essentials of salvation without falling victim to the "fables of human device."[1] Whereas those who embraced traditional church doctrine did so at the expense of human reason, Socinus thought his own individual theological ventures gave him clarity that was otherwise inaccessibly clouded by the traditions of the church.

This position, of course, was a stark reaction against the Roman Catholic Church, for it impinged upon the Roman church's monopoly on authority and set the individual readers in a position to determine authoritative teaching for themselves. Socinus even called upon believers to reject "every interpretation which is repugnant to right reason,"[2] a practice which he believed would lead to the rejection of much Catholic teaching and a restoration of the original purity of the Scriptures. For the Socinians, that purity included rejecting anything that could not be explained or understood by human reason, including all divine mystery. Like many movements in church history (such as Arianism), Socinus rejected the significance of the great tradition of Christianity and sought to develop his views apart from the influence of others.

Because Socinus and his followers elevated human reason so highly, they also held to a specific version of the sufficiency of Scripture that further undermined the authority of the clergy and the learned elite. The Socinian system did not reject human teachers altogether, however, as the Polish Brethren understood the need for the masses to learn from the literate. According to the Racovian Catechism, human teachers had four main purposes: (1) to help the illiterate or unlearned masses to understand Scripture; (2) to collect the various Scriptures into a logical argument; (3) to encourage people to act on what they know; and (4) to aid in dealing with the more difficult passages of Scripture. This low view of the Scriptures compared with human reason also led Socinus to renounce any nonbiblical terminology (such as "Trinity" or "original sin"), for to use such terminology, he argued, would be to introduce human traditions at the expense of the clear teaching of Scripture.

Unitarianism

Based on the concepts that the clear teaching of Scripture should suffice and tradition is irrelevant in all theological teaching, Socinus argued that the ecumenically accepted doctrine of the Trinity could not be defended. For one, the term never appears in Scripture — an undisputed point. Also, the very concept of a triunity (as most of his contemporaries referred to the doctrine) of personhood with a singularity of essence flew in the face of human reason. No one would dispute that a reading of the Old Testament demands monotheism, but Socinus and his followers did not account for the way the New

Testament authors include Jesus conclusively within the identity of the God of Israel.[3]

Despite his lack of formal training, Socinus did not shy away from the more academic arguments of theology. With an intellect that demonstrated a keen understanding of both the philosophical and the text critical[4] arguments of his day, Socinus waded into the discussion regarding the definition of the terms "person" and "essence" with confidence. According to the Socinians, the idea that those two terms could be used distinctly made a mockery of the biblical text. Rather, the term "person" should simply be defined as "an indivisible, intelligent essence," and, thus essence and person were interchangeable — to say that God is one essence means that he is one person, as Sabellius had suggested (see chapter 6). This definition led naturally to the concept of the radical oneness of God that has largely become synonymous with Socinianism. Unfortunately, Socinus failed to take into account both the biblical basis for the Trinity and the careful Trinitarian distinctions used by his medieval scholastic predecessors, most significantly Aquinas and Duns Scotus, both of whom demonstrated with great care that there is no logical difficulty in understanding God as both three persons and one simple undivided essence.

That unity of God also undergirded Socinus's Adoptionist view of Jesus of Nazareth. According to the Racovian Catechism, the Socinians did acknowledge some supernatural aspect of Jesus' birth, but they did not accept the traditional understanding of his divinity. Rather, Jesus, the man, was chosen by God for a special work. He was adopted and given a unique filling of the Holy Spirit adequate and necessary for that office, that of Redeemer.

For Socinus, this understanding of divine unity did not merely apply to the office of Christ; it also had serious ramifications for his understanding of the Holy Spirit, which Socinus argued was merely the "virtue or energy flowing from God"[5] without any distinct personhood. Thus, like the spirit of a man, the Spirit of God, or Holy

Spirit, simply referred to an aspect of the divine being, not a distinct person.

View of the Atonement

Given his understanding of the radical unity of God and, consequently, Jesus' merely human existence, Socinus's view of the atonement logically differed from commonly accepted views — especially that of Anselm and the Calvinist modification of Anselm's view. Because Jesus was not divine, Socinus argued that his death could not have been intended to make satisfaction (as Anselm argued) or to pay a penalty on behalf of other humans (as the Calvinists argued). Instead, Socinus understood Christ's death to serve as a way for God to model true love and devotion and to demonstrate the way of salvation. Jesus, then, provided the unique and divinely anointed model for humans to imitate. Because Socinus thought that the idea that Jesus was both God and man ended up compromising his humanity, he also suggested that seeing Jesus as merely human was of more comfort to believers. After all, if Christ was merely human and was resurrected, Socinus argued, it provided much more assurance of our own resurrection than if Christ triumphed over death as a supernatural being.

By the time of Socinus's death, Protestant discussions had begun to focus on the minutiae of the extent of the atonement Christ's death achieved. Rather than getting caught up in those discussions, Socinus provided a radically different concept of the atonement, one which did not need an answer for how Christ's death affected salvation or who it saved. According to Socinus, the death of Christ was indeed glorious and divinely orchestrated, but God did not die in the person of Jesus.[6]

Consequently, Socinus considered any discussion about the payment made by that death premature and misplaced. Socinus, or at least his contemporary followers, did, in places, allow for the resurrected Christ to take on added significance in God's ongoing divine governance of the cosmos. As the vindicated one, the resurrected Christ could, at least in the view of some Socinians, take an eternal role in God's kingdom. This modified view provides some added significance to Christ's death on the cross without shifting the overall teaching away from Socinus's atonement model.

In the end, the Socinian model of the atonement — even the modified versions of some of Socinus's followers — removes the necessity of the death of Christ and provides no method for dealing with the problem of sin, the central problem for humanity according to leading theologians from both the Catholic and Protestant traditions. According to the Socinian system, the same "benefits" provided by the crucifixion of Jesus could have been delivered in other ways, though the sheer dramatic effect of the method used would be difficult to duplicate.

Orthodox Response

Unlike many viewed as radical during the Reformation, Faustus Socinus avoided imprisonment and execution. Hostile reactions to his views forced Socinus to leave his family home in Siena and seek refuge in lands controlled by leaders who supported religious liberty. On several occasions, Socinus experienced persecution from unruly mobs, the last such incident occurring in Krakow, where he had lived for several years. On that occasion, Socinus was dragged from his house and injured badly. During his subsequent recovery, Socinus moved to a village outside of Krakow that provided more safety from such popular uprisings. He remained there until his death several years later.

Catholic Response

Thanks to the Catholic Church's heavy-handed response to the Reformation in the lands they still controlled, Socinus's teachings quickly became labeled as heretical and found their way onto the

Index of Forbidden Books. For the Catholic hierarchy, Socinianism served two major purposes. First, it confirmed the church's fears about making the Scriptures available to the laity. In the eyes of the Catholic leadership, the unlearned masses' having access to the Word of God could only lead to a "twisting" of Scripture that would undermine the historical teaching of the church — as Socinus aptly demonstrates. Europe had already witnessed the monstrosities of such an event with the anarchical destruction of Munster in 1534–35, a horror feared by Catholic and Protestant alike. Second, Socinus demonstrated the intellectual and theological extremes that could be reached without the stabilizing effects of the authority of tradition. For the Catholic Church, a rigid understanding of theological truth provided the only sure defense against such ungodly heresy. The Catholic Church officially condemned Socinianism as heresy in two different papal bulls. The first, declared by Pope Paul IV and titled *Cum quorundam* (1555) dealt more with the teachings of Lelio Socinus than of Faustus, though the two were nearly identical on the key aspects. The second condemnation, pronounced by Pope Clement VIII in 1603, was titled *Dominici gregis*.[7] These two bulls combined to condemn the Socinian tenets that denied the Trinity, the deity of Christ, the doctrine of original sin, the unique understanding of the sacraments, and the denial of the authority of tradition.

Protestant Response

The Protestant Reformers also condemned nearly every aspect of the Socinian system. For the most part, Poland and Transylvania were both dismissed as lands "owned" by the Radical Reformation, so the leading Protestant authorities did not fight Socinianism from a political stronghold — as they had done with other anti-Trinitarian theologies such as that espoused by Michael Servetus, who was executed in Geneva in 1553.

As was often the case in the midst of the Reformation, the leaders of the orthodox sects and those eventually labeled as heretics had a lengthy history. Lelio Socinus's travels during the 1550s provided him with numerous rich relationships with many of the Protestant leaders. During that time, Lelio Socinus shared some of his reservations about traditional doctrine, and several of those leaders responded with clear concern. Calvin, especially, warned Lelio against continuing in the line of "vain and fruitless" conjectures and inquiries, which he believed would result only in "severe suffering."[8]

By the time Faustus Socinus matured as a theologian, his uncle's acquaintances had apparently given up on the hope of providing any moderating support. While correspondence between Lelio and other Protestant leaders was abundant, the same cannot be said of Socinus. Rather, the Protestant response to Socinus and the full-fledged Socinian model was far more polemic in nature. The term "Socinian" quickly became a pejorative catchall for any theology with even a hint of anti-Trinitarianism. Across the spectrum of Protestantism — from those in the Lutheran camp to those in the Calvinist camp — Socinianism was renounced as heretical and extremely dangerous. After the Racovian Academy established its printing press in 1602, the Socinian doctrines began to spread, and the political and theological establishment found itself needing to respond.

The response of the English establishment serves as a prime example of the usual Protestant response to this system. The Racovian Catechism was first published in England at the beginning of the seventeenth century. The teachings were quickly denounced as heretical and banned by the Church of England. In 1612, Bartholomew Legate and Edward Wightman became the last two English people to be executed as heretics. Among the charges that led to their conviction was the charge that they held Socinian tenets. In 1614, King James ordered all copies of the Racovian Catechism burned with the hope of weeding out anti-Trinitarian theologies. The move did not work, and by the end of the seventeenth century, works written both in support and in condemnation of Socinianism abounded. The Racovian Catechism even found a new audience among the religious sects during the tumultuous seventeenth century.[9]

Contemporary Relevance

While the term "Socinian" has largely fallen out of use, Socinian doctrines continue to have influence. Most modern unitarian theologies trace their history either directly to Socinus or to other theologians who were directly influenced by Socinian teachings. In England, entire Christian groups bought into some aspects of Socinian theology during the late seventeenth and early eighteenth centuries. Additionally, the Socinian model of the atonement can still be found within more liberal Protestant theologies — both explicitly and implicitly.

By far the strongest legacy of Socinianism can be found in the elevation of human reason in the interpretation of Scripture. The central Socinian tenet of the authority of human reason as the final arbiter of truth — over against both human tradition and supernatural revelation — became one of the preeminent philosophical foundations of much of modern civilization. That foundational premise held sway for the better part of three hundred years. The influence of Socinus in that area simply cannot be ignored, and that influence was not limited to the philosophical world.

The question must be asked whether this theological system and its influence over modern Western thought can be harmonized with the teachings of Scripture that clearly move beyond human reason. In the end, the believer must decide what role human tradition and human authority will, should, or must play in the determination of orthodoxy. The hyperindividualized "me and my Bible" understanding of theology and biblical interpretation espoused by Socinus and the Socinian system has become commonplace within evangelical Protestantism. As J. I. Packer put it, "[Tradition] is not infallible, but neither is it negligible, and we impoverish ourselves if we disregard it."[10]

Discussion Questions

1. While Jesus' death is certainly an example of the highest form of human sacrifice, what do we lose if his death were *only* an example for us to emulate?
2. What are some ways that today's society allows faith to be determined and judged by autonomous human reason?
3. One of Socinus's major shortcomings was his insufficient view of the Trinity. Many today share Socinus's view that the doctrine of the Trinity is either nonsensical or irrelevant. In what ways does the Christian doctrine of the triune God positively impact our faith?

Further Reading

Franks, Robert S. *The Doctrine of the Trinity.* London: Duckworth, 1953.

Greig, Martin. "The Reasonableness of Christianity? Gilbert Burnet and the Trinitarian Controversy of the 1690s." *Journal of Ecclesiastical History* 44, no. 4 (1993): 631–51.

McLachlan, H. John. *Socinianism in Seventeenth-Century England.* London: Oxford Univ. Press, 1951.

Mortimer, Sarah. *Reason and Religion in the English Revolution: The Challenge of Socinianism.* Cambridge Studies in Early Modern British History. Cambridge: Cambridge Univ. Press, 2010.

CONCLUSION

The disadvantage of men not knowing the past is that they do not know the present. History is a hill or high point of vantage, from which alone men see the town in which they live or the age in which they are living.

— G. K. Chesterton, "On St. George Revivified"

Dwell on the past and you will lose an eye. Forget the past and you will lose both eyes.

— Russian Proverb

What are we to make of all these controversies? It is tempting to see the history of orthodoxy and heresy as proof that no one knows very much about God, and that any opinions work. If the church can become deeply divided over so basic a doctrine as whether Jesus is God, then it might be better to agree just to get along with one another and do the best we can. After all, Jesus did say that if a person loves God and loves others, then they are fulfilling all of the commandments. "Why," you may ask, "does it even matter if we believe the right things about God as long as we love God and other people?" Two brief responses to this objection are worth noting.

First, while it is certainly true that living doctrine out in love for God and others is important, Jesus also said that part of loving God is loving him with all of our minds, souls, and strength — that is, with our entire person. Believing right things about God is part of loving him, in the same way that it matters to you whether someone knows your interests, likes and dislikes, occupation, and past. And second, in order to love God we have to know who he is. When the Israelites were training their children, they referred to God by recalling the things he had done for them in the past. The God they worshiped was the God of Abraham, Isaac, and Jacob, and the one who had brought them out of Egypt in the exodus. They used specific phrases to specify who it was that they were worshiping. The orthodox under-standing of the Trinity and of Jesus Christ does something similar — it identifies who the God Christians worship actually is. Therefore, in order to love God, one must know who God is. In this way, right belief about God — orthodoxy — matters quite a bit.

Christians should agree that there exists a perfect orthodoxy in the mind of God; however, the proliferation of schisms, disagree-ments, and divisions throughout church history points to the fact that we as sinful and fallible humans are imperfect at agreeing pre-cisely on that orthodoxy. The general overview of the heresies and the church's orthodox responses in this book should make clear how messy the pursuit for theological truth can be.

However, there is room for mystery in Christian belief. We must remember that the entirety of what we think Christians *should* believe is not identical to what a person *must* believe to be saved. We believe in justification by faith in Christ, not justification by accuracy of doctrine. We are not saved by our intellectual preci-sion; we are saved by the grace of Jesus. That does not diminish the importance of correct doctrine, but rather allows it its proper place in glorifying the triune God, who graciously saves sinners because of the person and work of Christ.

As I hope has been clear in this book, the line between ortho-doxy and heresy has developed over time and through theological conflict, and the line between heterodoxy and heresy is blurry. That means we need lots of wisdom, discernment, and humility before we declare that someone has departed into full-blown heresy. At the same time, we should be clear in our minds on the nonnegotiables of Christian doctrine and belief.

The current climate of the church shows that Christians need to relearn the ability to care about right doctrine and have earnest doctrinal disagreements without shouting "heresy!" when we disagree. We need a more restrained definition of heresy drawing on the early church creeds. The Nicene Creed is a historic, globally accepted ecumenical creed that encapsulates the good news of the gospel into a short and rich summary. It covers the basic essentials of (1) who God is, (2) what God is like, and (3) how God saves.

If a believer authentically holds to the Nicene Creed, we should not call them a heretic, no matter how strongly we believe they are gravely in error on the details or on other doctrines. A good shorthand for heresy, then, is to ask, "Can they say the Nicene Creed and mean it without their fingers crossed?" If the answer is yes, they may still be wrong, and they may be heterodox, but we cannot call them heretics, because they fit within the bounds of historic Christianity.

Even with this narrow and confined definition of heresy, we should still discuss and debate with those whose beliefs are unhelpful. We can still say that their teachings are not a good application of Scripture to life and doctrine. But don't treat them as heretics. Treat them as brothers and sisters with whom we lovingly disagree. As the famous saying goes, "In essentials unity, in nonessentials liberty, and in all things love."

Rather than either of the two extremes — nothing is heresy on the one hand, and everything that I disagree with is heresy on the other — the church has continually confessed that heresy is that which deviates from the central teachings of the Christian faith, as expressed in the rule of faith and subsequently in the church's confessions. As such, Christians today would do well to recover the doctrinal precision of the early church before judging any belief as heretical.

Heresy is not located in one's beliefs about baptism, one's beliefs about the continuation of certain spiritual gifts, or one's beliefs about a specific view of the atonement. It is a specific and direct denial of any of the central beliefs of the Christian church about the deity and identity of the triune God and about the person and work of Jesus Christ.

Perhaps the best way to construct an opposite of "heresy" is not simply "right belief" — though, technically speaking, orthodoxy is the opposite of heresy. The category of "confession" is much more positive. Since even the demons have "right belief,"[11] it is appropriate to see confession as a joyful dependence on the gospel of Jesus Christ. As John Webster says, "To confess is to cry out in acknowledgement of the sheer gratuity of what the gospel declares, that in and as the man Jesus, in the power of the Holy Spirit, God's glory is the glory of his self-giving, his radiant generosity. Very simply, to confess is to indicate 'the glory of Christ' (2 Cor. 8.23)."[12]

An attitude of humble, charitable engagement stands in stark contrast to the spirit of theological conflict today. Rather than turning disagreement into division, we should contend for the truth with humility and grace. That's how Jesus treated us.

THE COUNCIL OF NICAEA AND THE NICENE CREED

Many of the chapters in this book reference Nicaea or Nicene orthodoxy. What we call the Nicene Creed is actually the product of two ecumenical councils—one in Nicaea in AD 325, and one in Constantinople in AD 381—and a century of debate over the nature of the relationship between the Father, the Son, and the Holy Spirit.

The Council of Nicaea was a watershed for the Christian church — shortly after Emperor Constantine legalized Christianity in 313, he convened the first ecumenical, fully representative, universally recognized council of the Christian church. There, the bishops discussed one of the most important questions that Christianity would ever have to face — what was the status of Jesus in relation to God? Everyone there agreed that Jesus was a divine being, but the Arians (see chapter 7) could not reconcile the idea that he was the same being as God the Father.

After a long and heated debate, the council decided that the evidence from the Bible and tradition lent itself much better to the belief that Jesus was God rather than a lesser being. They phrased this belief as follows: "[We believe] in one Lord Jesus Christ, the Son of God, begotten of the Father [the only-begotten; that is, of the essence of the Father, God of God], Light of Light, very God of very

God, begotten, not made, being of one substance with the Father; by whom all things were made [both in heaven and on earth]; who for us men, and for our salvation, came down and was incarnate and was made man; he suffered, and the third day he rose again, ascended into heaven; from thence he shall come to judge the quick and the dead."

Later, at the Council of Constantinople in 381, the bishops added a section to include the Holy Spirit as God as well: "[We believe] in the Holy Ghost, the Lord and Giver of life, who proceeds from the Father,[13] who with the Father and the Son together is worshiped and glorified, who spoke by the prophets."[14]

Although the Trinity had been a standard doctrine long before Nicaea, these two councils provided Christians with the language that they needed to discuss the Trinity and the authority to use the Trinity as a basis for evaluating orthodoxy. Thus, when I reference Nicaea or Nicene orthodoxy in this book, I am talking about the fact that the bishops of the era were concerned that any new theories about God or Christ needed to line up with the Nicene Council.

ANTIOCH AND ALEXANDRIA

Two Understandings of Christ

Of the four major Christian centers in early Christianity (Antioch, Alexandria, Constantinople, and Rome), Antioch and Alexandria produced some of the greatest theologians. Alexandria was known for names like Origen, Cyril, and Athanasius; Antioch for Nestorius and Theodore of Mopsuestia.

The two cities were natural rivals, partly because they were both large Mediterranean ports which controlled a lot of trade (think Boston and New York), and partly because they had very different ways of interpreting Scripture. Alexandria tended to produce more creative theologians who emphasized the spiritual. So when it came to Christ, Alexandrians wanted the church to endorse theories in which his divinity played a major role. They tended to favor theories in which Christ was spoken of as a single person (a "who") rather than the sum of his divine and human natures (the "whats"); sometimes this is referred to as a "Word-flesh" outlook, because Christ's godhood is the main focus and the human part is almost incidental. Heresies that sprang from Alexandria included Eutychianism, Monothelitism, and Apollinarianism.

Antioch, by contrast, was concrete, literal, and historical. Antiochene theologians wanted to emphasize that God had come down *as a human person* and walked on earth with us. As a result, Christ was not only God but also a fully functional human person with mind, will, desires, and all the embarrassing and nonpoetic parts of being human. Sometimes this is referred to as a "Word-man" outlook, because it emphasizes the entire human aspect of Jesus. However, the Antiochene view sometimes focused so heavily on Christ's historical human presence that his divinity became distant or abstract. Heresies that sprang from Antioch included Nestorianism.

NOTES

Introduction

1. Bruce Demarest, "Heresy," *New Dictionary of Theology* (Downers Grove, IL: InterVarsity Academic, 1988), 293.
2. Ibid., 292.
3. Ibid.
4. Tim Dowley, ed., *Introduction to the History of Christianity: First Century to the Present Day* (Minneapolis: Fortress, 2006), 109.
5. Irenaeus, *Against Heresies* 3.6.4.
6. Tertullian, *Prescription of Heretics* 7.
7. Tertullian, *Against Hermogenes* 8.
8. Clement, *Stromates* 7.15.
9. Cyprian, *Unity of the Church*, 3.
10. J. Wilhelm, "Heresy," in *The Catholic Encyclopedia* (New York: Robert Appleton Company), *http://www.newadvent.org/cathen/07256b.htm*.
11. Richard Muller, *Post-Reformation Reformed Dogmatics*, vol. 1, *Prolegomena to Theology* (Grand Rapids, MI: Baker, 2003), 422–23. Muller writes, "The first kind of error is a direct attack — such as those launched by the Socinians — against the divinity of Christ or the Trinity. The second is not a direct negation or an antithesis but rather an indirect or secondary error ultimately subversive of a fundamental — such as a belief in God that refuses to acknowledge his providence. The third category of error does not address fundamental articles directly or indirectly but rather involves faith in problematic and curious questions (*quaestiones problematicas et curiosas*) that do not arise out of the revealed Word — hay and stubble! — and that, because of their curiosity and vanity, constitute diversions from and impediments to salvation."
12. David Christie-Murray, *A History of Heresy* (Oxford: Oxford Univ. Press, 1989), 20.
13. For Bauer, heretical beliefs may not necessarily be false, and orthodox beliefs may not necessarily be true.
14. Demarest, "Heresy," 292.
15. Ignatius of Antioch, "Letter to the Philadelphians I:8," in *Early Christian Fathers*, ed. Cyril Richardson (New York: Simon and Schuster, 1995), 110.
16. See J. N. D. Kelly, *Early Christian Doctrines*, rev. ed. (New York: HarperCollins, 1978).
17. C. S. Lewis, "Learning in War-Time," in *The Weight of Glory: And Other Addresses* (New York: HarperCollins, 1949/2001), 58–59.

Chapter 1: Judaizers

1. Circumcision was a traditional Jewish practice, established by God in the Old Testament, in which the foreskin of the penis was cut off. By this practice, Jews distinguished themselves as a holy people, owned and protected by God. As you might imagine, this idea made some Jews more than a little proud.

2. See also Mark 7:19.

3. The *Greek-English Lexicon of the New Testament and Other Early Christian Literature* has "live as one bound by Mosaic ordinances or traditions, *live in Judean or Jewish fashion*." F. W. Danker, W. Bauer, W. F. Arndt, and F. W. Gingrich, *Greek-English Lexicon of the New Testament and Other Early Christian Literature*, 3rd ed. (Chicago: Univ. of Chicago Press, 1999), 478.

4. The closest parallel to the word comes right before it in the previous verse, where Paul says that Peter lives like a Gentile and does not "live like a Jew" (*zao Ioudaikos*). In fact, F. F. Bruce says this phrase is essentially identical to the word *ioudaizein*, "Judaize," at the end of the verse. F. F. Bruce, *The Epistle to the Galatians*, New International Greek Testament Commentary (Grand Rapids, MI: Eerdmans, 1982), 133.

5. For example, W. S. Campbell notes that it is found with the sense "to live as a Jew in accordance with Jewish customs" in Plutarch (*Cicero* 7.6), Josephus (*Jewish War* 2.17.10 §454), and Ignatius (*To the Magnesians* 10.3). W. S. Campbell "Judaizers," in *Dictionary of Paul and His Letters*, ed. Gerald F. Hawthorne and Ralph P. Martin (Downers Grove, IL: InterVarsity, 1993), 513. The word also appears once in the Septuagint, in Esther 8:17: "And many of the Gentiles were circumcised, and became Jews [*Ioudaizon*], for fear of the Jews."

6. Michael Bird, "Justification as Forensic Declaration and Covenant Membership," in *The Saving Righteousness of God: Studies on Paul, Justification, and the New Perspective*, Paternoster Biblical Monographs (Eugene, OR: Wipf and Stock, 2007), 114.

7. See Carl Trueman, "Am I Bovvered?" in *Fools Rush in Where Monkeys Fear to Tread: Taking Aim at Everyone* (New York: P&R Publishing, 2012).

Chapter 2: Gnostics

1. Stephen Patterson and Marvin Meyer, trans., *Gospel of Thomas*, 108, http://www.earlychristianwritings.com/text/thomas-scholars.html.

2. Everett Ferguson, *Backgrounds of Early Christianity*, 2nd ed. (Grand Rapids, MI: Eerdmans, 1993), 289.

3. With paraphrasing and adaptation for the ease of use of the reader. Carl B. Smith II, *No Longer Jews: The Search for Gnostic Origins* (Peabody, MA: Hendrickson, 2004), 11–12.

4. "The Holy Book of the Great Invisible Spirit," in *The Nag Hammadi Scriptures*, ed. Marvin Meyer (New York: HarperCollins, 2007), 254.

5. "On the Origin of the World," in Meyer, *Nag Hammadi Scriptures*, 206.

6. Ibid.

7. "The Nature of the Rulers," in Meyer, *Nag Hammadi Scriptures*, 193.

8. "The Second Discourse of the Great Seth," in Meyer, *Nag Hammadi Scriptures*, 480.

9. "The Gospel of Truth," in Meyer, *Nag Hammadi Scriptures*, 38.

10. Ibid., 37.

11. "The Secret Book of James," in Meyer, *Nag Hammadi Scriptures*, 28.

12. Henry Chadwick, *The Early Church*, rev. ed. (New York: Penguin, 1993), 35.

13. Edwin M. Yamauchi, *Gnostic Ethics and Mandaean Origins* (Piscataway, NJ: Gorgias Press, 2004), 28.

14. Irenaeus of Lyons, *Against Heresies* II:26, *http://www.newadvent.org/fathers /0103226.htm*.

15. Irenaeus of Lyons, *Against Heresies* IV:9, *http://www.newadvent.org/fathers /0103409.htm*.

16. Irenaeus of Lyons, *Against Heresies* V:3, *http://www.newadvent.org/fathers /0103503.htm*.

17. Clement of Alexandria, *Miscellanies* VII:3, *http://www.earlychristianwritings.com /text/clement-stromata-book7.html*.

18. Dan Brown, *The Da Vinci Code* (New York: Random House, 2003), 251.

19. Ibid., 266. There were a few groups where this was true. The Ebionites, of which we know very little (and mostly from Irenaeus), apparently believed that Jesus was only a good human being.

20. See *www.gnosis.org*.

21. From the official website of *The Secret* and *The Power*, *http://thesecret.tv/thepower/*.

22. For a good guide to how Gnosticism has affected American religion, see Ross Douthat, *Bad Religion: How We Became a Nation of Heretics* (New York: Simon and Schuster, 2012).

Chapter 3: Marcion

1. Principally from Irenaeus, Tertullian, and Hippolytus.

2. Allegedly he had gotten in trouble with the church before Rome. It was said his own father, the Bishop of Sinope, excommunicated him, but this cannot be confirmed. See Philip Schaff, *History of the Christian Church*, vol. 2 (1858; Peabody, MA: Hendrickson, 2006), 484.

3. Henry Chadwick, *The Early Church* (London: Penguin, 1993), 39.

4. W. H. C. Frend, *The Rise of Christianity* (Philadelphia: Fortress, 1984), 212.

5. Irenaeus, *Against Heresies* III.3.4.

6. Frenz, *Rise of Christianity*, 213.

7. Tertullian, *Against Marcion* 1.19.

8. The Pastoral Epistles were excluded, apparently because Paul attacks early forms of Gnosticism. "Gal. 3:16–4:6 was cut because of its references to Abraham, his sons, and his promises, and 2 Thess. 1:6–8 because God was not concerned with 'flaming fire' and punishment." Frend, *Rise of Christianity*, 215.

9. This caused him to cut from the Bible anything in the Gospels that resembled the Old Testament, such as the birth narratives. In his book *Antitheses* he made a list of what he saw as contradictions between the Old and New Testaments. He saw the God of the Old Testament as the creator of a miserable world, as the author of evil, and as nothing like the Father of Jesus.

10. Stephen Nichols, *For Us and for Our Salvation* (Wheaton, IL: Crossway, 2007), 28.

11. Tertullian, *Against Marcion* 3:8.
12. Taken from Geoffrey W. Bromiley, *Historical Theology: An Introduction* (Grand Rapids, MI: Eerdmans, 1978), 29.
13. Tertullian, *Against Marcion* 1.3.
14. Eric Osborn, *Tertullian, First Theologian of the West* (New York: Cambridge Univ. Press, 1997), 93. See Tertullian, *Against Marcion* 1.14.
15. Ibid., 97.
16. Tertullian, *Against Marcion* 1.27. Marcion was reputed to be "a most holy teacher" (1.28). "Come, then, if you do not fear God as being good, why do you not boil over into every kind of lust? ... God forbid, you say with redoubled emphasis. So you do fear sin, and by your fear prove that He is an object of fear Who forbids sin."
17. See Tertullian, *Against Marcion*, Books III, IV, and V for more details.
18. Tertullian, *Against Marcion* 1:38.
19. Tertullian, *Against Marcion* 4.6.
20. Irenaeus, *Against Heresies* 1.27.2–3.
21. Ibid.
22. See Tertullian, *Against Marcion*, Book IV for fuller details.
23. Richard Dawkins, *The God Delusion* (Boston: Houghton Mifflin, 2006), 31.
24. Bruce Shelley, *Church History in Plain Language*, 2d ed. (Nashville: Thomas Nelson, 2008), 64.
25. Schaff, *History of the Christian Church*, vol. 2, 483.

Chapter 4: Docetists

1. Paul L. Gavrilyuk, *The Sufferings of the Impassible God: The Dialectics of Patristic Thought*, Oxford Early Christian Studies (New York: Oxford Univ. Press, 2006), 79.
2. *Gospel of Peter* 4.10.
3. J. N. D. Kelly, *Early Christian Doctrines* (Peabody, MA: Prince Press, 2004), 141.
4. Taken from Gavrilyuk, *Sufferings of the Impassible God*, 81. More of this can be found in "The Second Discourse of Great Seth," in *The Nag Hammadi Scriptures*, ed. Marvin Meyer (New York: HarperOne, 2007), 473–86.
5. Ibid.
6. Taken from Philip Schaff, *Creeds of Christendom*, vol. 2 The Greek and Latin Creeds (1931; Grand Rapids, MI: Baker, 1993), 11–12. For full text, see Ignatius, "The Epistle of Ignatius to the Trallians," in *Ante-Nicene Fathers*, vol. 1 (reprinted, Peabody, MA: Hendrickson, 1995), 69–70. (Hereafter *ANF*.)
7. Ignatius, "Epistle of Ignatius to the Symrnaeans," in *ANF*, vol. 1, 88.
8. Polycarp, "The Epistle of Polycarp," in *ANF*, vol. 1, 34.
9. Ibid, 35. 1 Peter 2:24; 1 John 4:9.
10. Incarnation is the doctrine that the Son of God was conceived in the womb of the Virgin Mary and that Jesus is true God and true man.
11. For more details see Irenaeus, "Against Heresies," 5.14.2, in *ANF*, vol. 1, 541.
12. Stephen Nichols, *For Us and For Our Salvation* (Wheaton, IL: Crossway, 2007), 26.
13. Rudolf Bultmann, "Paul's Demythologizing and Ours," in *The Writings of St. Paul*, ed. Wayne A. Meeks and John T. Fitzgerald, 2nd. ed. (New York: Norton, 2007), 602.

14. Machen, *Christianity and Liberalism*, 92.
15. Thomas F. Torrance, *Incarnation: The Person and Life of Christ*, ed. Robert T. Walker (Downers Grove, IL: InterVarsity Academic, 2008), 185.

Chapter 5: Mani

1. Geo Widengren, *Mani and Manichaeanism* (Great Britain: George Weidenfeld and Nicolson, 1965), 23–24.
2. "The Vision of the Angel: Cologne Mani-Codex 3–5; 11–44," in Andrew Welburn, *Mani, the Angel, and the Column of Glory: An Anthology of Manichaean Texts* (Edinburgh: Floris Books, 1998), 14–15.
3. Widengren, *Mani and Manichaeanism*, 26.
4. Ibid., 41–42.
5. "The Seal of the Prophets: Turfan Fragment T II D 126," in Welburn, *Mani, the Angel, and the Column of Glory*, 214.
6. Widengren, *Mani and Manichaeanism*, 118, 133.
7. Welburn, *Mani, the Angel, and the Column of Glory*, 35.
8. "Cosmic Evolution: The Seizure of the Light: From al-Nadim, *Fihrist*," in Welburn, *Mani, the Angel, and the Column of Glory*, 176.
9. "Primal Man's Sacrifice: Theodore bar Konai, *Book of Annotations*," in Welburn, *Mani, the Angel, and the Column of Glory*, 181.
10. J. N. D. Kelly, *Early Christian Doctrine* rev. ed. (New York: Harper Collins, 1978), 14.
11. Jason BeDuhn, *The Manichaean Body: In Discipline and Ritual* (Baltimore: Johns Hopkins Univ. Press, 2000), 130.
12. "Songs of the Living Self," in BeDuhn, *Manichaean Body*, 154; see also 231.
13. "The Seduction of the Archons: Mardan Farukh, Refutation That Destroys All Doubt," in Welburn, *Mani, the Angel, and the Column of Glory*, 196.
14. BeDuhn, *Manichaean Body*, 21.
15. Ibid., 200.
16. Interestingly, the God particles took different forms depending on the actions of the human toward the environment during his lifetime. Widengren says, "He who mowed the sown field would himself be born again as an ear of corn, whilst he who killed a mouse would in future life be a mouse, and so on." Widengren, *Mani and Manichaeanism*, 97. This partly explains why Manichaean Elect were forbidden from procuring food for themselves, and why they pleaded their innocence to their food before eating it: "It was not I who killed thee, O melon."
17. Ephrem, *The Second Discourse to Hypatius against Mani and Marcion and Bardaisan*, trans. C. W. Mitchell, *http://www.tertullian.org/fathers/ephraim1_2_hypatius2.htm*.
18. Augustine, *The Confessions*, trans. Maria Boulding (New York: New City Press, 2001), III:9.
19. Augustine, *Contra Faustum*, IV:1, *http://www.newadvent.org/fathers/140604.htm*.
20. Augustine, *Contra Faustum*, IV:2, *http://www.newadvent.org/fathers/140604.htm*.
21. Augustine, *Contra Faustum*, XIV:3–6, *http://www.newadvent.org/fathers/140604.htm*.

22. Augustine, *Contra Faustum*, XXIX:2, *http://www.newadvent.org/fathers/140604 .htm*.

23. Augustine, *Contra Faustum*, V:5, *http://www.newadvent.org/fathers/140604.htm*.

24. BeDuhn, *Manichaean Body*, 116.

25. Augustine, *Contra Faustum*, V:2, *http://www.newadvent.org/fathers/140604.htm*.

26. However, in recent years a new religious leader has emerged calling for the reestablishment of Manichaeanism: see *www.manichaean.org*.

Chapter 6: Sabellius

1. Henry Chadwick, *The Early Church*, rev. ed. (New York: Penguin, 1993), 86.

2. Ibid., 87.

3. This particular reading is found only in the Septuagint, which was the standard Christian Old Testament at the time.

4. Jaroslav Pelikan, *The Christian Tradition: A History of the Development of Doctrine*, vol. 1, *The Emergence of the Catholic Tradition (100–600)* (Chicago: Univ. of Chicago Press, 1971), 177.

5. Tertullian, *Against Praxeas* I:7, *http://www.newadvent.org/fathers/0317.htm*.

6. In fact, Origen, one of the main Trinitarian theologians in the orthodox party, developed a model of the Trinity that placed Jesus as a "secondary god," which hinted at a demigod even though Origen understood this to refer to Jesus' position within the Trinity. The model was later refined, and Origen was temporarily excommunicated long after his death. See J. N. D. Kelly, *Early Christian Doctrines*, rev. ed. (New York: Harper Collins, 1978), 128.

7. Kelly, *Early Christian Doctrines*, 123.

8. This is quoted by Tertullian, who never really addresses the issue. However, the introduction of creeds helped alleviate the problem — the content of the faith was condensed into a form that common people could memorize and recite every time they went to worship. Tertullian, *Against Praxeas* I:3, *http://www .newadvent.org/fathers/0317.htm*.

9. Kelly, *Early Christian Doctrines*, 124.

10. Philip Schaff, ed., *Socrates and Sozomenus Ecclesiastical Histories* I:5, *http://www .ccel.org/ccel/schaff/npnf202.ii.iv.v.html*.

11. Tertullian, *Against Praxeas* I:10, *http://www.newadvent.org/fathers/0317.htm*.

12. Tertullian, *Against Praxeas* I:22, *http://www.newadvent.org/fathers/0317.htm*.

13. Both sets of terms have made their way into Christian language in the West, and so both are included here.

14. The Old Testament and some of the deuterocanonical books feature a personified Wisdom that the early church fathers often associated with Christ.

15. Athanasius later used the same argument against the Arians.

16. Tertullian, *Against Praxeas* I:8, *http://www.newadvent.org/fathers/0317.htm*.

17. Tertullian, *Against Praxeas* I:22, *http://www.newadvent.org/fathers/0317.htm*.

18. David S. Yeago, "The New Testament and the Nicene Dogma: A Contribution to the Recovery of Theological Exegesis," in T*he Theological Interpretation of Scripture: Classic and Contemporary Readings*, ed. Stephen E. Fowl (Oxford: Blackwell, 1997), 88.

19. C. S. Lewis, *The Weight of Glory and Other Addresses*, rev. ed. (New York: Harper Collins, 1980), 58.

Chapter 7: Arius

1. Church historian Kenneth Latourette remarks, "Origen was so outstanding a mind, so radiant a spirit, and so stimulating a teacher and author, that for more than a century after his death he profoundly moulded the minds of Christian thinkers." Kenneth Scott Latourette, *A History of Christianity: Beginnings to 1500* (Peabody, MA: Prince Press, 2005), 151.

2. Roger E. Olson, *The Story of Christian Theology: Twenty Centuries of Tradition and Reform* (Downers Grove, IL: InterVarsity, 1999), 143.

3. Ibid., 144.

4. Arius, "Arius' Letter to Alexander of Alexandria," in *Trinitarian Controversies*, Sources of Early Christianity, ed. and trans. William G. Rusch (Minneapolis: Fortress, 1980), 25.

5. Ibid.

6. J. N. D. Kelly, *Early Christian Doctrines*, rev. ed. (New York: Harper Collins, 1978), 227.

7. Arius, "Letter to Eusebius," in *Documents of the Christian Church*, ed. Henry Bettenson and Chris Maunder, 3rd ed. (New York: Oxford Univ. Press, 1999), 43.

8. Kelly, *Early Christian Doctrines*, 229.

9. Justo Gonzalez, *A History of Christian Thought*, vol. 1, *From the Beginnings of the Council of Chalcedon*, rev. ed. (Nashville: Abingdon, 1992), 266–67.

10. Taken from Philip Schaff, *The Creeds of Christendom*, vol. 1 (1931; Grand Rapids, MI: Baker, 1993), 29.

11. Athansius, "Four Discourses against the Arians," in *Nicene and Post-Nicene Fathers: Second Series* (herafter *NPNF*), vol. 4, trans. Cardinal Newman, ed. Philip Schaff and Henry Wace, reprint (Peabody, MA: Hendrickson, 1995), 306.

12. Taken from Alister E. McGrath, *Historical Theology: An Introduction to the History of Christian Thought* (Malden, MA: Blackwell, 1998), 49–51.

13. Harold O. J. Brown points out, "[Adolf] Harnack observes that Arius 'is a strict monotheist only with respect to cosmology; as a theologian, he is a polytheist.'" Harold O. J. Brown, *Heresies: Heresy and Orthodoxy in the History of the Church* (Peabody, MA: Hendrickson, 2003), 115.

14. For details on Athanasius's exegetical arguments concerning the divinity of the Son, see "Four Discourses against the Arians," in *NPNF*, 303–447.

15. Athanasius, *Orations against the Arians* 1:1.

16. Athanasius, "Defense of the Nicene Creed," V. Athanasius writes, "For though all things be said to be from God, yet this is not in the sense in which the Son is from Him; for as to the creatures, 'of God' is said of them on this account, in that they exist not at random or spontaneously, nor came to be by chance, according to those philosophers who refer them to the combination of atoms, and to elements of similar structure, nor as certain heretics speak of a distinct Framer, nor as other again say that the constitution of all things is from certain Angels; but, in that whereas God is, it was by Him that all things were brought into being, not being before,

through His Word; but as to the Word, since He is not a creature, He alone is both called and is 'from the Father'; and it is significant of this sense to say that the Son is 'from the essence of the Father,' for to nothing originate does this attach."

17. Athanasius, *Contra Arianos* III.
18. Athanasius, *Contra Arianos* II:70.
19. Quoted in Olson, *Story of Christian Theology,* 164–65. See also Alvyn Pettersen, *Athanasius* (Harrisburg, PA: Morehouse, 1995), 175.
20. Brown, *Heresies,* 154.
21. James B. Torrance describes the impact of the Trinity on worship as follows: "As we reflect on the wide varieties of forms of worship ... we can discern two different views.

    "*The unitarian view.* Probably the most common and widespread view is that worship is something which we, religious people, do — mainly in church on Sunday. We go to church, we sing our psalms and hymns to God, we intercede for the world, we listen to the sermon (too often simply an exhortation), we offer our money, time and talents to God. No doubt we need God's grace to help us do it. We do it because Jesus taught us to do it and left us an example of how to do it. But worship is what *we* do before God ... Indeed this view of worship is in practice unitarian, has no doctrine of the mediator or sole priesthood of Christ, is human-centered, has no proper doctrine of the Holy Spirit, is too often non-sacramental, and can engender weariness ...

    "*The trinitarian view.* The second view of worship is that it is the gift of participating through the Spirit in the incarnate Son's communion with the Father. It means participating in union with Christ, in what he has done for us once and for all, in his self-offering to the Father, in his life and death on the cross. It also means participating in what he is continuing to do for us in the presence of the Father and in his mission from the Father to the world. There is only one true Priest through whom and with whom we draw near to God our Father ... It takes seriously the New Testament teaching about the sole priesthood and headship of Christ, his self-offering for us to the Father and our life in the union with Christ through the Spirit, with a vision of the Church as the body of Christ ... [God] lifts us up out of ourselves to participate in the very life and communion of the Godhead, that life of communion for which we were created." James B. Torrance, *Worship, Community and the Triune God of Grace* (Downers Grove, IL: InterVarsity, 1997), 20–22.
22. Athanasius, *On the Incarnation* 10.

Chapter 8: Apollinarius

1. Harold O. J. Brown, *Heresies: Heresy and Orthodoxy in the History of the Church* (Peabody, MA: Hendrickson, 2003), 160.
2. J. N. D. Kelly, *Early Christian Doctrines,* rev. ed. (New York: Harper Collins, 1978), 291.
3. Brown, *Heresies,* 163.
4. Stephen Nichols, *For Us and for Our Salvation* (Wheaton, IL: Crossway, 2007), 103.

5. Prominent early church scholar J. N. D. Kelly observed, "If it is objected that this makes Him different from ordinary men, Apollinarius had no hesitation in agreeing." Kelly, *Early Christian Doctrines*, 292.

6. Roger E. Olson, *The Story of Christianit Theology: Twenty Centuries of Traditions and Reform* (Downers Grove, IL: InterVarsity Academic, 1999), 189.

7. Although Gregory of Nazianzus refused to acknowledge it, most modern scholars recognize that Apollinarius was likely deeply influenced by the Christologies of Origen and Athanasius. Ibid., 189. In fact, Apollinarius was a young friend to Athanasius. See Kenneth Scott Latourette, *History of Christianity: Beginnings to 1500*, rev. ed. (New York: HarperCollins, 1953; Peabody, MA: Prince, 2006), 165.

8. Apollinarius, "Fragment 107," cited in J. N. D. Kelly, *Early Christian Doctrines*, 291–92. Apollinarius wrote, "The flesh, being dependent for its motions on some other principle of movement and action (whatever that principle may be), is not of itself a complete living entity, but in order to become one enters into fusion with something else. So it united itself with the heavenly governing principle [the Logos] and was fused with it … Thus out of the moved and the mover was compounded a single living entity — not two, nor one compound of two complete, self-moving principles."

9. Kelly, *Early Christian Doctrines*, 292.

10. Latourette, *History of Christianity*, 165.

11. Quoted in Anthony Meredith, *The Cappadocians* (Crestwood, NY: St. Vladimir's Seminary Press, 1995), 44.

12. Gregory of Nazianzus, "To Cledonius against Apollinaris (Epistle 101)," in *Christology of the Later Fathers*, ed. Edward Hardy (Louisville: Westminster John Knox, 1984). This quote can also be found in Gregory of Nazianzus, *Nicene and Post-Nicene Fathers*, vol. 7, ed. Philip Schaff and Henry Wace (Peabody, MA: Hendrickson, 1995), 440.

13. Ibid.

14. Ibid.

15. Ibid., 439–40.

16. See B. B. Warfield, "The Emotional Life of Our Lord," in *The Person and Work of Christ* (Phillipsburg, NJ: Presbyterian and Reformed, 1970). Warfield begins his argument for the full humanity of Jesus by examining the emotions displayed by our Lord. He shows how the compassion, indignation, and joy displayed by Christ not only prove his complete humanity, but also give us a necessary glimpse into the nature of Jesus as a man.

17. John A. T. Robinson, *Honest to God* (Louisville: Westminster, 1963), 65–66.

Chapter 9: Pelagius

1. Harold O. J. Brown, *Heresies: Heresy and Orthodoxy in the History of the Christian Church* (Peabody, MA: Hendrickson, 1988), 201.

2. See Rodney Stark, *Rise of Christianity: How the Obscure, Marginal Jesus Movement Became the Dominant Religious Force in the Western World in a Few Centuries* (San Francisco: Harper Collins, 1997).

3. Peter Brown, *Augustus of Hippo: A Biography*, rev. ed. (Berkley: Univ. of California

Press, 2000), 341. "Pelagius reached his peak, in Rome, in a world where cultivated Christian laymen exercised more influence than any time previously."

4. This invasion prompted Augustine to write *City of God*.

5. Augustine, *Confessions* 10.40.

6. Pelagius, *Letter to Demetrias* I.

7. Pelagius, "Letter to Demetrias," in *Theological Anthropology*, Sources of Early Christian Thought, ed. and trans. J. Patout Burns (Philadelphia: Fortress, 1981), 53.

8. Pelagius, *Letter to Demetrias* VIII.

9. J. N. D. Kelly, *Early Christian Doctrines*, rev. ed. (New York: Harper Collins, 1978), 357.

10. This is what Augustine alleged Caelestius summarized in *On the Proceedings of Pelagius* 23.

11. Roger E. Olson, *The Story of Christian Theology: Twenty Centuries of Tradition and Reform* (Downers Grove, IL: InterVarsity, 1999), 270.

12. "Augustine *Ep.* clvii (to Hilarius)," in *Documents of the Christian Church*, 4th ed., ed. Henry Battenson and Chris Maunder (New York: Oxford Univ. Press, 2011), 61.

13. Augustine, *On the Merits and Forgiveness of Sins, and on Baptism of Infants* 1.2.

14. Augustine, *To Simplician* 18.

15. Alister E. McGrath, *Historical Theology: An Introduction to the History of Christian Thought* (Malden, MA: Blackwell, 1998), 83.

16. "We must realize that [Pelagius] believes that neither our will nor our action is helped by divine aid. He believes that such help is given only to the capacity to will and work, the only member of this trio which he says comes from God. Hence he believes that this capacity which God himself has placed in human nature is weak while the other two which he claims for us are so stable, strong, and self-sufficient that they do not need God's aid. Thus he believes that God does not help us to will, that he does not help us to act, that he helps us only to be able to will and to act." Augustine, *On the Grace of Christ* V.6.

17. Augustine, *On the Grace of Christ* V.6.

18. Augustine, *On the Grace of Christ* VI.7.

19. Augustine, *On the Grace of Christ* VIII.9.

20. Augustine, *On Nature and Grace* 2.

21. Albert C. Outler, "Introduction," in *Confessions and Enchiridion*, Christian Classics Ethereal Library, *http://www.ccel.org/ccel/augustine/confessions.html*.

22. Augustine, *On Nature and Grace* 6. Augustine's theology was not perfect, of course. There were some dark corners to his soteriology, such as the requirement of baptism to wash away original sin. The unavoidable conclusion that he did not shy away from then was that anyone who died without baptism must go to hell, even babies, albeit with the lightest punishment. B. B. Warfield observed that the Protestant Reformation was basically the revolt of Augustine's doctrine of grace against his doctrine of the church. See David F. Wells, *Turning to God* (Grand Rapids, MI: Baker, 1989), 84.

23. Robert L. Reymond, *A New Systematic Theology of the Christian Faith* (Nashville: Thomas Nelson, 1998), 469.

24. Augustine, *On Rebuke and Grace* 38.

Chapter 10: Eutyches

1. Quote taken from Aloys Grillmeier, S.J., *Christ in Christian Tradition*, vol. 1, *From the Apostolic Age to Chalcedon (451)*, trans. John Bowden (Atlanta: John Knox, 1975), 479.

2. Roger E. Olson, *The Story of Christian Theology: Twenty Centuries of Tradition and Reform* (Downers Grove, IL: InterVarsity, 1999), 224.

3. Philip Schaff, *History of the Christian Church*, vol. 3, *Nicene and Post-Nicene Christianity* A.D. 311–590, reprint (Peabody, MA: Hendrickson, 2006), 736.

4. Olson, *Story of Christian Theology*, 226.

5. Stephen Nichols, *For Us and for Our Salvation* (Wheaton, IL: Crossway, 2007), 106.

6. See Theodoretus, "Dialogues: The 'Eranistes' or 'Polymorphous' of the Blessed," in *Nicene and Post-Nicene Fathers: Second Series*, vol. 3, trans. Blomfield Jackson, ed. Philip Schaff, reprint (Peabody, MA: Hendrickson, 1995), 160–244.

7. Ibid., 160.

8. "The Admissions of Eutyches," in *Documents of the Christian Church*, ed. Henry Batteson and Christ Maunder (New York: Oxford Univ. Press, 2011), 51.

9. See "Letter XXI: From Eutyches to Leo," in *Nicene and Post-Nicene Fathers: Second Series*, vol. 12, trans. Charles Lett Feltoe, ed. Philip Schaff, reprint (Peabody, MA: Hendrickson, 1995), 32–34.

10. See "Letter XXVIII: To Flavian Commonly Called 'the Tome,'" in *Nicene and Post-Nicene Fathers: Second Series*, vol. 12, trans. Charles Lett Feltoe, ed. Philip Schaff, reprint (Peabody, MA: Hendrickson, 1995), 39–43.

11. Schaff, *History of the Christian Church*, vol. 3, 739.

12. It took the presence of imperial guards to keep both schools in the same building and to keep the peace.

13. Leo, "Letter XXVIII: To Flavian Commonly Called 'the Tome,'" 40.

14. Docetism was a heresy that held that Christ was only divine, while his humanity was only an appearance. For more information see chapter 4: "Docetism."

15. Cyril, "Cyril's Letter to John of Antioch," in *The Christological Controversy*, Sources of Early Christian Thought, trans. and ed. Richard A. Norris Jr. (Philadelphia: Fortress, 1980), 141–42.

16. "The Definition of Chalcedon," in Batteson and Maunder, *Documents of the Christian Church*, 54, emphasis in original.

17. Many of Dioscorus's allies admitted their errors and they were restored in fellowship. Only Dioscorus remained adamant in his aversion to any language of two natures of Christ. He was deposed from his position as Bishop of Alexandria and subsequently excommunicated.

18. Nichols, *For Us and for Our Salvation*, 113.

19. Ibid., 116.

Chapter 11: Nestorius

1. A good summary of the two views, as well as an example of how Antiochene and Alexandrian interpretations clashed at Ephesus, can be found in Donald Fairbairn, "Grace and the Central Issue of the Christological Controversy," in *Grace and Christology in the Early Church* (Oxford: Oxford Univ. Press, 2003).

2. J. N. D. Kelly, *Early Christian Doctrines*, rev. ed. (New York: Harper Collins, 1978), 317–26.

3. Jaroslav Pelikan, *The Christian Tradition: A History of the Development of Doctrine*, vol. 2, *The Spirit of Eastern Christendom (600–1700)* (Chicago: Univ. of Chicago Press, 1977), 74. See Hebrews 2:10–18.

4. Wilhelm Baum and Dietmar W. Winkler, *The Church of the East: A Concise History* (London: Routledge Curzon, 2003), 22–23.

5. Once they learned of Nestorius's intentions, the Arians themselves set it ablaze. John McGuckin, *St. Cyril of Alexandria and the Christological Controversy* (New York: St. Vladimir's Seminary Press, 2004), 24.

6. Ibid.

7. Ibid., 37.

8. Ibid., 33.

9. Kelly, *Early Christian Doctrines*, 311.

10. The Latin word for suffering is *passio*, which is why Easter Week is called Passion Week.

11. Nestorius, *The Bazaar of Heracleides*, trans. G. R. Driver and Leonard Hodgson (Oxford: Clarendon, 1925), 9. Nestorius wrote *The Bazaar of Heracleides* after the Council at Ephesus in a vain attempt to clear his name. In the book, Nestorius lists a number of heresies that he wishes to refute, but these two appear most often, and he accuses Cyril of being "compelled to join either the Arians or Manichaeans in such a way as to admit either that he suffered not naturally any one of these things or only in illusion and in fiction." Ibid., 39.

12. Nestorius, *Bazaar of Heracleides* 58.

13. Ibid., 73.

14. McGuckin, *St. Cyril of Alexandria*, 130.

15. Nestorius, *Bazaar of Heracleides* 47: "Thou wilt confess aloud with us that there are not two Gods the Words or two Sons or two only begottens, but one, and so on with all the rest of them."

16. Henry Chadwick, "The Christological Debate I: To the First Council of Ephesus (431)," in *The Church in Ancient Society: From Galilee to Gregory the Great* (Oxford: Oxford Univ. Press, 2001), 12.

17. Ibid., 13. According to Chadwick, the Roman government passed a law limiting the number of monks in Alexandria to six hundred and ordered them not to interfere any longer in secular affairs.

18. Cyril of Alexandria, *Five Tomes against Nestorius* (Oxford: James Parker, 1881), 70.

19. Ibid., 77.

20. Ibid., 97.

21. It is sometimes called the communication of idioms, from the Latin phrase *communicatio idiomatum*.

22. Kelly, *Early Christian Doctrines*, 324.

23. McGuckin, *St. Cyril of Alexandria*, 47.

24. Ibid., 64.

25. Ibid., 60.

26. Wilhelm Baum and Dietmar W. Winkler, *The Church of the East: A Concise History* (London: Routledge Curzon, 2003), 23–25.

27. Kelly, *Early Christian Doctrines*, 327.
28. Ibid., 311–16.
29. For the text of a Nestorian monument in China, see "East Asian History Sourcebook: Ch'ing-Tsing: Nestorian Tablet: Eulogizing the Propagation of the Illustrious Religion in China, with a Preface, Composed by a Priest of the Syriac Church, 781 A.D." *http://www.fordham.edu/halsall/eastasia/781nestorian.asp*.

Chapter 12: Socinus

1. Racovian Catechism, 16.
2. Ibid., 18.
3. On which, see Richard Bauckham, *Jesus and the God of Israel: God Crucified and Other Studies on the New Testament's Christology of Divine Identity* (Grand Rapids, MI: Eerdmans, 2008).
4. While this arena of academic thought had not fully developed by Socinus's day, discussions regarding the content of the original text and the trustworthiness of a given reading were commonplace. The most common discussion of this nature centered around the *Comma Johanneum* (1 John 5:7), a text directly linked to the doctrine of the Trinity. Interestingly, Socinus does not use textual criticism to refute 1 John 5:7, instead opting for a different interpretation of the text altogether.
5. Racovian Catechism, 285.
6. Though, it is important to note that with the exception of the Lutheran strand of the Reformation, most theologians (in keeping with the Christian tradition) were quite careful when attributing death to Jesus Christ. That is, they were clear that Jesus Christ absolutely did die, but he did so according to (or *qua*) his human nature. The divine nature of Jesus Christ did not die, so it is improper to say without qualification that "God died."
7. Both of these official responses were published prior to the publication of the Racovian Catechism.
8. *Letters of John Calvin*, no. 30.
9. Certainly some of this focus stemmed from the fact that the term "Socinianism" could be applied to just about any nontraditional theology. Thus, the outcry against Socinianism was not always against the actual teachings of Fausto Socinus. However, enough of the tenets remained central that the opposition generally still applied.
10. J. I. Packer, "Upholding the Unity of Scripture Today," *JETS* 25 (1982): 414, *http://www.etsjets.org/files/JETS-PDFs/25/25-4/25-4-pp409-414_JETS.pdf*.
11. See James 2:19. It is interesting to see what the enemies of Jesus Christ, the demons, thought and said about him in the Gospels. It is fascinating because what they say repeats what the rest of the Bible proclaims about who Jesus Christ is:

    "'What do you want with us, Son of God?' they shouted. 'Have you come here to torture us before the appointed time?'" (Matt. 8:29).

    "What do you want with us, Jesus of Nazareth? Have you come to destroy us? I know who you are — the Holy One of God!" (Mark 1:24; Luke 4:34).

    "You are the Son of God" (Mark 3:11).

    "'You are the Son of God!' But he rebuked them and would not allow them to speak, because they knew he was the Messiah" (Luke 4:41).

"What do you want with me, Jesus, Son of the Most High God? I beg you, don't torture me" (Luke 8:28; Mark 5:7).

Prior to the demons' declarations about Jesus is his command over them. In each of the passages, the demons are not even permitted to voice their beliefs without the permission of Jesus, the sovereign God. When they are permitted to speak, they acknowledge his cultural identity, his divinity, and his power over their each and every move. They acknowledge him as Lord, Son of God, the Holy One of God — and they shudder before him. The demons know that Jesus has come to earth from heaven to judge them (Luke 4:34), destroy the kingdom of darkness (Gen. 3:15; Rom. 16:20), disarm the demonic order (Col. 2:15), and set captives free from sin and death (Rom. 6:23; 8:2). Calling him "Son of God" is a clear declaration of Jesus' divinity (Matt. 26:63–64; John 5:17ff; 10:33–36), and the phrase "Holy One of God" is never used to describe anyone but God (Jer. 50:29; Isa. 30:11). Who is holy but God alone (1 Sam. 2:2)?

12. John Webster, "Confession and Confessions," in *Confessing God: Essays in Christian Dogmatics* (New York: T&T Clark, 2005), 71.

13. Later, Western theologians added "and the Son," while Eastern theologians kept the original text. This contributed to the split between Eastern and Western Christianity later.

14. Philip Schaff, *Creeds of Christendom*, vol. 1, section 8, *http://www.ccel.org/ccel /schaff/creeds1.iv.iii.html*.